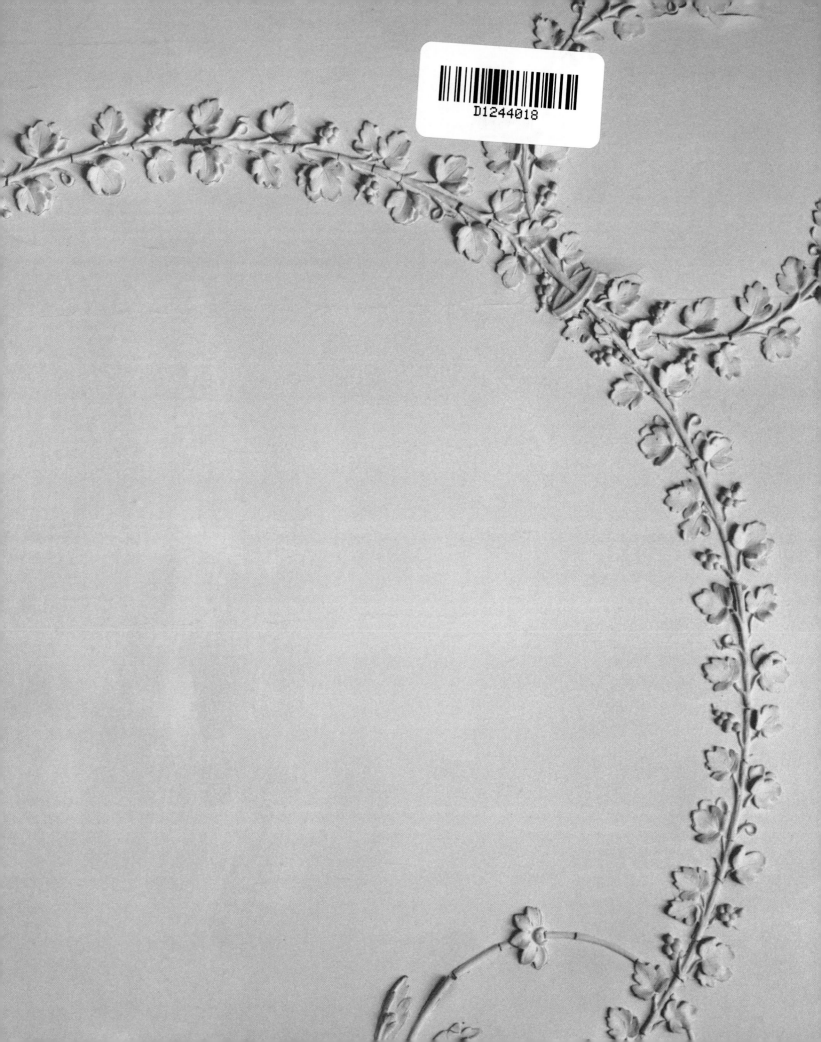

THE REBIRTH OF
AN ENGLISH COUNTRY HOUSE
ST GILES HOUSE

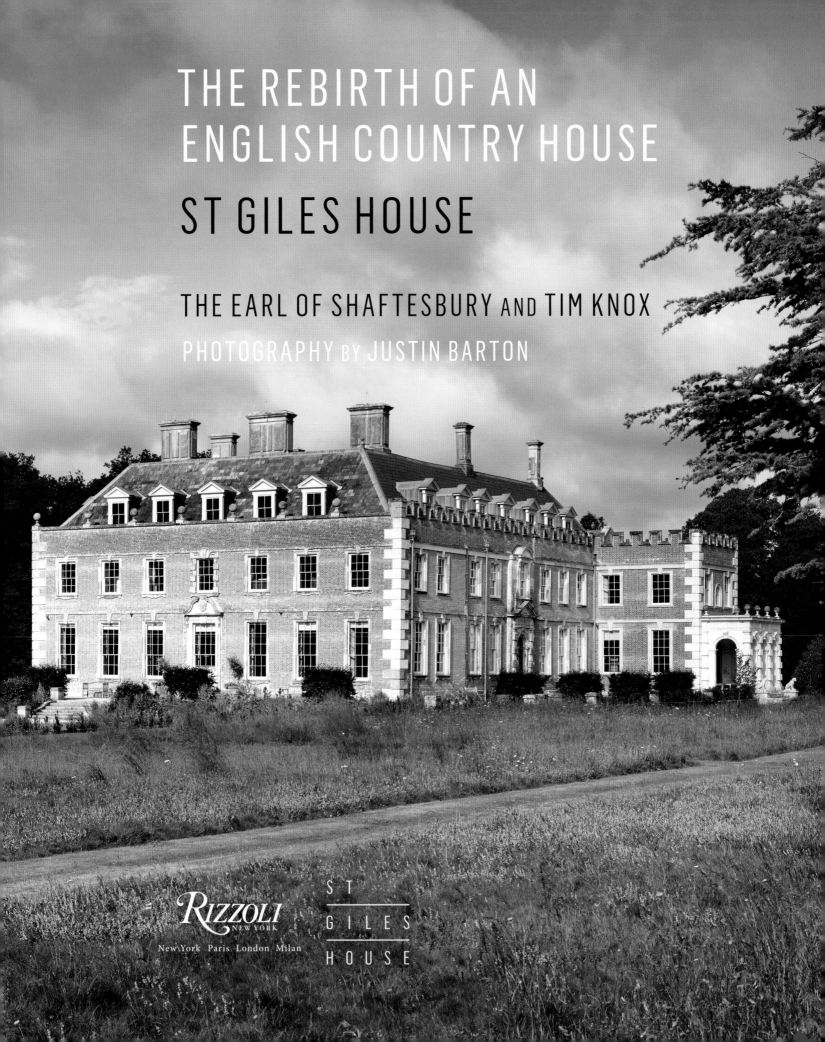

THE REBIRTH OF AN ENGLISH COUNTRY HOUSE

ST GILES HOUSE

THE EARL OF SHAFTESBURY AND TIM KNOX

PHOTOGRAPHY BY JUSTIN BARTON

RIZZOLI
NEW YORK

New York Paris London Milan

ST GILES HOUSE

THIS BOOK IS DEDICATED TO MY FATHER
AND TO MY BROTHER, ANTHONY

CONTENTS

FOREWORD

The revival of the Wimborne St Giles estate, and the restoration of St Giles House itself, is one of the most remarkable and memorable cases with which I have been involved in my time as a Historic Buildings Inspector. The change in the fortunes of the house is one of the most dramatic I have seen in a historic building of this importance, as it has been brought back from the brink of collapse. When I first visited the estate, the semi-derelict condition of St Giles House was a conservation *cause célèbre* on a national level, its rescue despaired of by eminent architectural historians of the time. Few Grade I buildings fall into such disrepair, particularly those that are an ancestral home at the heart of a landed estate. St Giles House seemed to hang in the balance at the start of the twenty-first century. As a result, relations between English Heritage (now Historic England) and the Shaftesbury Estate had become strained, but the intervention of Christina, Countess of Shaftesbury, proved critical to establishing a more positive relationship. This then allowed constructive discussions on the restoration of the house to begin, albeit that they were prompted by the interest of a commercial developer in obtaining permission for development on the estate. Nevertheless, this provided a catalyst for our organisation to engage with the estate, although the scale of development being proposed seemed a high price to pay for the restoration of the house.

It was the subsequent involvement of Anthony Ashley-Cooper, who was then heir to the title and estate, which marked a pivotal change in the direction of the discussions and put the restoration of the house and landscape at the heart of the process. We were tremendously encouraged by Anthony's enthusiasm and commitment—not just to saving the house, but ultimately to re-occupying it as the Shaftesbury family home. Anthony's untimely death was a devastating loss to the estate and a major setback to the restoration plans, all the more tragic because he never lived to see the realisation of his dreams. However, his formative influence on the direction of the restoration project should not be underestimated. Anthony's positive approach contributed much to the relationship between English Heritage and the Shaftesbury Estate, and we were very impressed with his growing sense of responsibility towards the house in particular. This gave us an increasing optimism for the future of St Giles House and Park which we would not have believed possible only a few years previously. His vision for the estate is now in the process of being realised.

History has proved Anthony's legacy to have been both positive and lasting. However, it could not have been accomplished without his younger brother taking on the baton of both the management of the estate and the challenges of St Giles's restoration with an equal degree of commitment and vision. Our earliest discussions on the restoration of St Giles had revolved around a considerable amount of 'Enabling Development' [a type of planning permission granted in exceptional circumstances that would not otherwise be given, normally in order to raise funds for a special project—in this case to save an important historic building] being necessary to accomplish it. This makes it all the more extraordinary that it has been achieved—and in such an exemplary fashion that it has won some of the most prestigious national restoration awards—from resources generated by the estate. Apart from a limited amount of grant aid provided by English Heritage for emergency repairs to the house in the early stages of discussions, public funding has not been provided for the restoration of the house. That initial grant aid was critical, however, in buying the house more time—by literally keeping parts of it standing—whilst its long-term future was debated and options for reusing it were discussed. Ultimately, the risk of the estate being permanently fragmented or spoilt by excessive development was thankfully averted through the commitment and vision of two brothers who were both Earls of Shaftesbury.

The phrase 'triumph over tragedy' is over-used, but this is one case where it can genuinely be applied. St Giles House is now widely recognised as a textbook restoration case study. At one level, its restoration illustrates the power of historic buildings to survive adversity, overcome physical damage, neglect, and the fluctuating fortunes of their owners, and be revitalised in spirit as well as physically repaired. Despite its poor condition, St Giles House, and all that it represented for the family, inspired two brothers to struggle against almost overwhelming obstacles to save it, so it could continue as their family home. The restoration of St Giles House, and the revival of the estate in general, demonstrates the resilience of great historic houses, and their ability to rise above the circumstances of individual owners and endure through the generations. In a wider context, the project has allowed the work of many generations of skilled craftsmen and artisans to survive for future generations to enjoy and marvel at; and it has provided opportunities for their modern-day counterparts to continue to use those traditional skills in bringing the house back to life. As with all such projects, there hasn't always been complete agreement about the best way to achieve every aspect of the restoration, but overall the project has been remarkably harmonious. Nick Ashley-Cooper faced a steep learning curve when he assumed responsibility for the estate, with all of its crumbling historic structures and neglected gardens. However, the speed with which he grasped difficult conservation issues and gained confidence in how he wanted his vision for the house to be achieved was remarkable. Over the years, it has been noticeable that Nick has developed a very personal philosophy towards the house's restoration. This has evolved to take a more minimal approach which does not seek to restore, or reproduce, every original historic element. Rather than presenting the interior of the house in an immaculate state, it retains elements of faded grandeur and the memory of its former decline—nowhere more successfully than in the dining room, where walls remain partially unplastered to convey a sense of its former condition and reveal evidence of earlier features. This allows visitors to appreciate the journey that the house has travelled in the last fifty years, and is in many ways more illuminating than presenting the house in a fully restored state. It marks out the restoration of St Giles as different to that of other, similar, houses and is something that will be particularly appreciated by future generations.

Perhaps the most unique and poignant aspect of the project is how it reflects the intertwined fortunes of St Giles House and the family who built it and have owned it for many generations. Through his achievement of restoring the house, there is a strong sense that the 12th Earl has revived the fortunes of the Shaftesbury estate and its family, and he has received glowing accolades and prestigious awards for saving the house and reviving a respected estate. The building that once felt gloomy, abandoned and decaying, is now a home filled with light, colour and activity. Its formerly silent rooms now reverberate with family life and children's voices. Finally, and fittingly, though, the Earls of Shaftesbury have returned home, and it has been a privilege to be a part of that story.

JENNY CHESHER
Inspector of Historic Buildings and Areas at Historic England

INTRODUCTION

As you enter St Giles Park, you turn a corner and St Giles House comes in to view, sitting peacefully in its parkland setting. It has a presence that is instantly captivating. During my childhood its beauty was tinged with sadness. The house was not lived in, and it felt unloved. Crumbling walls, boarded up windows and battle scars from previous periods of demolition were clearly visible on all sides. It seemed as if the world had moved on, leaving the house behind to fall slowly into ruin.

As a child, I often wondered about what fate lay in store for the house. The topic was not one we discussed openly as a family. My father rarely shared details of family history with my brother or me. His challenges with the house had been painful for him and were not experiences he was readily able to open up about. As a result, we almost never went inside, and as I grew up, the house remained a mystery to me. My parents, my brother and I lived on the other side of the village in a lovely country house, so it was easy to avoid thinking about it. Furthermore, as a second son, I knew that it was never going to become my problem, as my older brother, Anthony, would inherit it. I consciously parked any concerns I had about its future at the back of my mind and set about finding a path for myself elsewhere.

Fate would prove me wrong though, and after a series of tragedies I would end up inheriting St Giles House in 2005, aged 26. Amidst the turbulence of those years, the issue of what to do with the house became a central focus of my attention. It had been added to the Heritage at Risk register by Historic England, the public body that looks after England's historic environment, and discussions with them had been ongoing. Whilst significant progress had been made towards understanding the building and its condition, no decision had yet been reached about what should be done with it.

In the proceeding years, I spent a lot of my time getting to know the house—exploring the rooms; looking through books, letters and photographs; and reading stories about my ancestors. For the first time I allowed myself to delve deeply into its history. Reading about my family and imagining their lives at the house inspired me. Over the centuries they had filled the house with love, adapting it to the changing times and making it their own. It was humbling to be part of something that had been around for so long, and it became a huge motivation for me to want to do something about its demise.

After meeting my wife, Dinah, and starting a family together we began to discuss the possibility of moving in to a small part of the house to turn it into a home again. We wanted to build a stronger connection with the house and to develop ideas for its future. We were also excited about the idea of raising a family there and the adventure of bringing the house back to life. Thanks to Dinah's courage and willingness to take a leap of faith with me, she agreed to the idea of moving in. In March 2012 we became the first generation to live there since my great-grandfather, who died in 1961. The house welcomed us with open arms, and it wasn't long before we began to develop plans to restore further parts. The years that followed have been the most rewarding time of our lives.

NICK ASHLEY-COOPER
12th Earl of Shaftesbury

opposite Nicholas and Dinah Ashley-Cooper, 12th Earl and Countess of Shaftesbury.

AN INHERITANCE

I HAD BEEN LOOKING FORWARD TO THE WEEKEND OF 14 MAY 2005. It was the first time my brother Anthony would visit me in New York and it coincided with a DJ gig I was playing in one of Manhattan's most popular nightclubs, Avalon. I had been living in New York for three years, working first in a nightclub called Arc (previously Vinyl) as a manager, then as a promoter, and finally DJ of my own party called Robots. At that time, music was my life, a passion I had developed from a young age. After getting my first set of turntables at sixteen I was determined to make it as a DJ, and it was through the growing popularity of Robots that I finally had the platform I needed to realise that ambition. The night of 14 May I would be playing with my friend, internationally renowned DJ Chris Liebing.

To make things even more exciting my other brother Fred had decided to join us and as our sister, Cecilia, already lived in New York, all four siblings would be together. It was rare for us all to be in the same location at that time, as we were living separate lives, with very different careers. My sister was a corporate lawyer; my older brother Fred worked in tel-evision as a director. (Fred and Cecilia are children from my mother's first marriage.) Anthony was a trained accountant who had also started to assume responsibilities for the family estate. We were very close as siblings and always supported each other in our various pursuits.

Anthony and I were two years apart in age and had grown up together. Early on we went to the same schools and shared many of the same friends and also a love for music. As teenagers we went to different schools, but we always remained close. I was the more rebellious and liked to push the boundaries—much to the exasperation of my parents and teachers—and he was more responsible. As a younger son of an aristocratic family, I had grown up with the understanding that the family estate would be my brother's, and that I would have to find my path elsewhere. That lack of expectation

Nicholas Ashley-Cooper, 12th Earl of Shaftesbury, in the Handel Room at St Giles House in 2010, before the restoration work begins.

shaped me as much as the presence of it shaped Anthony. I remember early on feeling relieved that I would not have to look after the family home, St Giles House, which was uninhabited and falling down.

The village we grew up in was quiet and rural, and as an adolescent it felt like the end of the world, where nothing much happened. I couldn't wait to be out exploring new places. The freedom of my circumstance enabled me to get away, but my brother always remained close to home and kept his eye on St Giles and his responsibilities there.

It had been a turbulent time leading up to that weekend as my father, who had gone missing in November 2004, had recently been found dead and his last wife had admitted to playing a hand in his death along with her brother Mohammed. They claimed it was an accident, although it was clear there had been foul play, and they were later both convicted of his murder. Aside from the shock, there was a degree of relief that his body had been found after months of no news. It enabled us to bring him home and bury him in a dignified way, which brought closure to a very sad chapter for the family. Anthony and I had spoken often during this time. My father was an alcoholic and suffered from huge mood swings and periods of depression. Towards the end of his life the situation had become increasingly volatile. There had been the real concern, given his fragile state of mind, that he would take the whole estate off the cliff. Thankfully my brother and mother, along with the estate manager, Philip Rymer, and the Trustees, were able to avoid any such catastrophe by ensuring the safe passage of the estate to my brother. My strategy, which involved either speaking very directly to my father about his issues or refusing to speak to him at all in protest at his behaviour, had little effect. There was simply no way to influence him and make him seek help. He was too far down the road to turn back. We all felt a very deep sadness and pity for him.

My father inherited the estate and house in 1961, at the age of twenty-two, from his grandfather, as his father had died when he was only eight. The lack of a father figure and the burden of the estate at a young age had a significant impact on him. His grandfather, the 9th Earl of Shaftesbury, born in 1875, was a late Victorian and had grown up in a different era. He did his best to look after my father but it was, by all accounts, a distant and formal relationship. There was little to no emotional support at the time my father inherited, and it was assumed that someone in his position would be perfectly fine.

Added to this, the immediate post-war period had been a very tough time for custodians of large country houses. Many houses were in poor condition having been used for different purposes during the two world wars, and hundreds were demolished by owners who saw no future in their upkeep. St Giles was a military infirmary during the First World War and a girls' school (which relocated from London) during the Second World War. Following this, the house was open to the public for a brief spell for teas and tours, overseen by my grand-aunt Lettice, whom I remember very fondly, although this failed to generate much income.

When my father inherited St Giles House, it needed huge investment to tackle years of wear and tear and dry rot, a form of wood decay caused by a species of fungi which had already caused significant damage to the interiors. Faced with a monumental task my father did not abandon St Giles, but instead embarked on an ambitious plan to try and save the building by reducing it in size. The project, which he began in the early 1970s, was about making it a more practical house to live in and returning it to its eighteenth-century form, which was inspired by the eighteenth-century engravings of the house by Thomas Vivares and B. Pryce which hung outside his office.

However, after four years of continuous work and with still plenty left to do to make the house habitable, he was forced to abandon the project. A costly divorce and a challenging economic climate had dried up funds, and he began to see the house as an impossible job that was in danger of swallowing up the whole estate. Holes caused by the demolition work were hastily covered up, shutters were drawn, and the building was left in limbo.

It was during this time he met and married my mother,

and my brother and I were born, which would prove to be a welcome distraction. My parents focused on creating a home for us at Mainsail Haul, the house my father grew up in, and St Giles was put on hold. Looking back now, I feel his failure to make St Giles work was a turning point for him and, although we never spoke about it, I know it must have weighed heavily on his mind. Later, through my own work on the house, I would come much closer to understanding my father and his relationship with St Giles. It has helped me come to terms with what happened and brought me much closer to him in death than I ever felt when he was alive. I used to feel anger towards him for the demolition and destruction he wreacked on the house, but I now see a lot of his work as brave and visionary. I feel sorry that he can never see the part he has played in saving the house and giving it a future. Despite the difficulty that he put the house in, he never gave up on it completely and in fact moved the estate office into its basement in the early 1980s, which gave the house a lifeline during the next few difficult decades.

On that weekend of 14 May I had intended, as much as possible, to forget about what had happened to my father and spend time with my siblings and celebrate with them. I was excited to show Anthony, who was now 11th Earl of Shaftesbury, my life in New York.

That evening we all went out and had dinner together before heading over to the nightclub. I was playing first, before Chris who was the headline act. However, it was normal for me to stay on until the end and support him. During the set I remember glancing over to my brother Anthony who had been staying close by in the DJ booth. For him it was the first time he had seen me play to a large crowd, and it was a great feeling to have him and my other siblings there. After a few hours he complained of feeling slightly unwell and wanted to head home to our sister's apartment where he was staying. It didn't strike me as anything unusual, and I just put it down to the fatigue you would expect from jetlag and a long day walking around Manhattan.

I got home in the early hours and fell asleep immediately. My phone rang after what felt like a short time and it was Cecilia, who sounded alarmed and asked me to come quickly, as Anthony had been taken ill. There was something in the tone of her voice that worried me, and I remember running through scenarios in my head on the way to meet them in the taxi. When I arrived I saw Fred and Cecilia in a huddle on the sidewalk, comforting each other. They were both visibly upset, and when I approached them they told me that they had received news that Anthony had died. The feeling was one of shock and disbelief. We were all led into the hospital and taken to a room where Anthony was lying. I felt numb and unable to comprehend what I was seeing. We phoned my mother and explained to her what was happening, and she immediately set about finding tickets to fly over.

It's hard to describe that day, and a large part of it still seems a blur to me now. I remember at one point walking around Manhattan on my own trying to comprehend the events that had unfolded, but a large part of me couldn't process it and didn't want to. My brother had woken up that morning as usual, and without any warning he suffered a heart attack while watching TV. The doctor's autopsy report found nothing abnormal and nothing that could explain the cause of death. The closest we got to a diagnosis was Sudden Adult Death Syndrome (SADS). He had just embarked on the career he had been waiting for his whole life, the earldom and responsibility for the estate, and it had all been cruelly taken away from him in an instant.

The fact that we were all there in New York meant that we were close by to support each other through the ordeal. That support got us through those dark days, which became filled with the logistics of preparing to take Anthony home and organising the funeral service for him at Wimborne St Giles. It was during one cab ride at that time, as I was talking with Cecilia, that it dawned on me I was now the 12th Earl of Shaftesbury. It was hard to come to terms with this, knowing that I was now the only surviving heir of this long family history.

INTERVENING YEARS

It was very clear to me that I needed to be back home supporting my mother and thinking about what I was going to do with the house and the estate. I immediately started planning how and when I would move back. The idea of going to business school was something I had flirted with previously, although not very seriously. It was suggested to me by a friend of my brother Fred, who had studied for a Masters in Business Administration (MBA) in New York. At the time, I was thinking about my future and whether making it as a DJ was a suitable long-term career path, and any prospect of studying felt a long way off as things were going well. Now the reality of taking over the family estate made business school feel like an imperative. I knew it was impossible for me to carry on DJ-ing professionally while managing my responsibilities on the estate, so I came to terms with the fact that my passion would eventually have to take a back seat.

During the next number of months I juggled staying up late DJ-ing and getting up early to study for exams, and was fortunate to secure a place at the London Business School to do an MBA. I left New York in the summer of 2006, and although my Robots parties went on for another year, it eventually became too difficult to manage from afar and we closed it down. It was the end of an era for me and for my musical career in New York, a time that had given me many good experiences and friends.

London Business School felt like a new chapter. As well as providing a great platform for my future working life and a host of lifelong friends, it allowed me to gather my thoughts on what had happened and what I was going to do next. The turbulence of the previous years had been a lot to digest, and I needed some space to come to terms with it all.

The south-east side of St Giles House during the demolition works in the 1970s. The two large holes on the south side covered by metal sheets are where two-storey Victorian bay windows were removed. Render has been carefully removed from the building's exterior to reveal the original brick. To the left, the top of the nineteenth-century South Tower has been removed leaving an exposed ridge line and a temporary roof for protection.

There had been sensationalist press stories on the demise of my father and the misfortune of the family. I had always been incredibly proud of my family history, and I was determined to show that we were not defined by this tragedy.

In 1985, when Anthony and I were both young boys, my parents took us to Westminster Abbey for the centenary of the death of the social reformer and philanthropist the 7th Earl of Shaftesbury and we listened to a moving address by the Archbishop of Canterbury. This was the first time I realised how important the 7th Earl had been for so many people. It always inspired me to know that he was part of our family. When I became the Earl of Shaftesbury, I started to delve deeper into the family history and built a very strong connection to it. I read the biography of the 1st Earl by Keith Haley and became completely engrossed in his life and his friendship with John Locke. Then I read how Locke had overseen the tutoring of the 3rd Earl, who rose to become a philosopher in his own right. It brought St Giles and the family history alive in a way I hadn't fully appreciated before.

During this time, I also began my first forays into St Giles House. It's hard to explain those moments, because it seems almost incredible, looking back now, that I had virtually no knowledge of the house at all. The only room I knew was my father's study, which was the Ante-room on the ground floor, but accessed via a very narrow flight of stairs from the basement, which housed the estate office. Once or twice we had come up as children to see him there and stare out of his window at the beautiful view across to the lake. However, the house was shuttered up, and my father never offered to take either my brother or me around.

It had become a very sad-looking place, in poor condition, but it still had a magical quality about it. The setting in the park was always breathtaking. The stories that had been passed down about life at the house from other family members portrayed it as a very happy family home.

The main part of the house had no heat or built-in electricity. Light through the principal rooms came from light bulbs attached to cable hung from the ceiling. All the principal ground-floor rooms could therefore be lit up by a single switch, which electrified a run of cable that went from room to room. The rooms on the bedroom floor had no light at all, so to see them, one either had to use a flashlight or fight your way to a window to try and open a shutter. A vivid memory I have was when I was exploring one of the bedrooms with a flashlight when the battery started to run out. In a moment of panic, I realised that unless I found my way back to the basement office I could be stuck in the house for a very long time trying to find my way out. I dashed back as quickly as I could, grateful to reach the office just as the light flickered out.

The initial searches revealed a house in complete disarray—with furniture, debris, dust and destruction in almost every room. Many of the rooms had props holding up beams, and in several areas plaster was stripped back to bare brick, revealing some impressive holes. In the White Hall you could see from the roof down to the basement, with large sections of the room missing. There was a makeshift gutter system carrying water internally through a part of the house and expelling it out of a hole in the building where the North Tower had been demolished. The roof had been leaking in several areas, evidenced by buckets positioned around the attic. Parts of the house felt dangerous, as if they might collapse at any moment.

Added to that, there were mountains of paperwork to be sorted through. Some days I would head to my father's study to be confronted with his desk full to the brim with correspondence and photos, and cabinets with files, some of them decades old. The knowledge that I was the only one who could sort through it all weighed me down.

Home reminded me of my childhood and everything I thought I was leaving behind, so there was a lot of emotional baggage for me to sort out there. My colleagues at business school were looking at careers in finance or consulting, or setting up their own companies in the city. For a long time that seemed a more plausible route for me to take rather than leave all that opportunity behind and stay down in Dorset.

However, as time went on I became more engrossed in work on the estate, and I started to build a strong connection to the house. Three documents in particular were very influential. First, the amazing work on the house by

John Cattell and Susie Barson from English Heritage (now Historic England), who had written a study on the house and its architectural development in 2003. This work became my bible, and I read it over many times. The second was a condition report from April 2003 by Philip Hughes, a Chartered Building Surveyor, building conservation expert and Society for the Protection of Ancient Buildings scholar, who outlined the major structural issues that were facing St Giles House and some of the important surrounding buildings. It was an essential piece of work that got me thinking about the project, and crucially it was how I got to meet Philip Hughes, who later became a central figure in the restoration work. The last was a complete history of the garden and landscape at St Giles House by Suzannah Fleming, which would form the basis of much of the restoration of the park. This work documented historical research carried out between October 2004 and the end of December 2005, and was compiled in a report in 2006.

In 2009 things started to move in a more focused way. That summer I had started to look at what to do with the books in the library. Some of the oldest and most valuable volumes still at St Giles House were part of the library of the 3rd Earl of Shaftesbury, and it was obvious they were important and in need of some attention. The books themselves were partly on shelves and partly on the floor. Some of the shelves were broken, and many looked in a precarious state.

I was given the name of book specialist Anthony Payne, who came to see me one morning to discuss how we could tackle the situation. After an hour or so, he came out looking a little overwhelmed at the state of everything. He suggested that I carefully clean the books, return them to the shelves, and then call him back. I followed his instructions, and over a period of three months we cleaned and put all the books back on the shelves. At the same time we cleared out the library of all the furniture and items that had piled up there. Payne returned and helped me reorganise the books, grouping the 3rd Earl's and the 7th Earl's collections in two separate sections. We then filled in the gaps with the rest of the books, in chronological order. It turned out to be a hugely therapeutic exercise, and it felt we were claiming back a room in the house. The feeling permeated through to the estate office, still located in the basement, where the team had been managing for years with little to no progress upstairs, and everyone seemed buoyed by what was happening.

The year 2009 also saw a renewed focus on looking at potential sources of funding for the house. I picked up conversations with Historic England that were started in 2002–3 by my mother and brother and temporarily halted following my brother's death in 2005. St Giles House is a Grade I–listed building on the National Heritage List for England, which is the highest level of listing for historic buildings in the United Kingdom. With this comes a huge amount of oversight and control by Historic England, with strict limitations on what you can do to the house and how you do it. St Giles had also been on the Historic England 'Buildings at Risk' register since its inception in the early 1990s. Therefore, there was considerable concern about the house's future and pressure was on us to come up with a solution.

The focus at that stage was on raising funds through creating some kind of housing development. However, the land around the estate is all within a conservation area, which makes obtaining development permission very difficult. So the discussion had shifted to exploring options for Enabling Development, which was a way of securing development on a site that would otherwise not be given permission. To obtain this there are numerous hurdles to overcome, and progress was extremely slow.

In parallel with these discussions we had been working on an agreement with Natural England, the government body that advises on the natural environment, to put parts of the estate into stewardship for various conservation initiatives in return for funding towards the historical features in the park, which were in very poor condition. The process required us to create a Parkland Plan, which was written by Chris Burnett Associates with input from Historic England and published in October 2010. This highlighted the major landscape features and historical elements in the park and included sections on hydrology, topography, plants and wildlife. The project proved successful, and we were lucky to be awarded significant grant aid towards the restoration of the park, which is mentioned later in the book.

Another important part of 2009 was that my brother and sister arranged for photographer and friend Justin Barton to come into the house and take photographs of the rooms without my knowing. This operation was carried out over the summer, with the results given to me as a surprise at Christmas that year. The photographs revealed a beauty in the house that I hadn't fully appreciated before. Suddenly, objects I had been walking past countless times were captured and brought to life in a magical way. Pieces of cornice, doorframes, broken bits of plaster and fragments of wallpaper became the focus. It is those details that we are now so finely attuned to when we do our restoration work. It convinced me that I needed Justin by my side for future projects on the house. It has been a wonderful relationship that has carried right through to the present day and is the reason that this book is now possible.

The final part of 2009, which really set the wheels in motion, was the idea to start looking at creating some accommodation in St Giles House. The lack of progress with Enabling Development had left me with a restlessness to do something. I knew it was impossible to make serious headway when I wasn't living on site. In order to make a big change I needed to live there and to call it home. I had met my now wife, Dinah, two years previously. Together we decided it would be a great moment to move into the house and create our own home.

Without her by my side I would not have been brave enough to take that leap. However, as a joint endeavour the prospect excited us. We approached it in an adventurous, slightly naive way, undaunted by the fact that our combined experience of building work was restoring the kitchen in our London flat. In our heads, we were imagining taking over two or three rooms, and running around with buckets to catch the water coming through the ceiling.

When thinking about whom to engage to do the job, the natural person to turn to was Philip Hughes, who had written his condition report in 2003. There was no one who knew more about the house or the issues we were about to face. In

December 2009 we met, and I explained my plans to him. We got on very well and made quick progress. He convinced me to take on a bigger slice of the building than I had at first envisaged. This included the principal floor, bedchamber floor, and external work relating to the remaining part of the south wing and South Tower. The area was one of the worst-damaged parts of the house due to the rainwater seeping through the remaining part of the South Tower, which had a temporary roof cover following its partial demolition in the 1970s. It also happened to be the most practical site for accommodation, as it contained previous bedrooms and the room sizes were generally smaller and more habitable. Therefore, by creating our accommodation, we would also be rescuing one of the worst affected parts of the building.

It would be a mistake to think the restoration of St Giles House was a fully-conceived and resolved idea from the start. In fact, it was a constantly moving beast, and real momentum built once we were in the house and knew what we were up against. That first step was crucial though, as focusing on a section of the house for accommodation had freed us from the psychological barrier of looking at the whole building and deciding where to begin.

THE HOUSE

PHASE 1

THE FIRST PHASE OF WORK ON SITE STARTED IN January 2011. It coincided with the birth of our first child, Anthony. The preceding year had been taken up with meetings, honing the plans and getting the right permissions in place to begin the work. It also involved appointing Ellis & Co. as the main contractor to do the work. They were specialist historic building contractors and their team was professional and experienced.

My thinking on central heating had evolved a great deal, and I saw there was an opportunity to embrace renewable technology as a way to reduce the running costs of the house and become more environmentally friendly. This involved installing a ground-source heating system with pipes running out along the bed of the lake (which would give heat to about a third of the house), a solar thermal heating system on the roof to top up the domestic hot water supply, and a solar photovoltaic panel array in our walled garden to produce electricity. The three components would completely update the antiquated system that had been put in by my great-grandparents when they last modernised the house about a hundred years earlier. I learned much later, through stories from the girls who had stayed at St Giles during the war when the house was a school, that it had always been freezing—in fact one letter referred to it as the 'North Pole'. I am sure this was a common problem in old country houses, but it is certainly a source of satisfaction that we can now heat the place to a comfortable living temperature, and quite economically. Much of this I owe to our estate plumber, Nigel, who carried out all the plumbing work single-handedly.

The south wing was partially demolished in the 1970s. The roofline crenellations set back from the main block, to the right, were added during the Phase 1 works, to complete the South Tower that had been reduced in height during the 1970s. The new crenellations were carved in the 1970s with the intention of using them, but the work was not completed. They were subsequently left out on the south terrace and exposed to the elements for thirty years. When they were dug out, they had become weathered and blended in well with the original stone.

THE ROOF

The house has a variety of roof structures with pitched and flat roofs, lanterns and internal gutter arrangements. The pitched roofs were covered in slates, and the flat roofs were covered in either lead or felt. A number of holding repairs, including re-felting the lantern roofs, had been undertaken to stabilise the roof and prevent water from leaking into the building over the preceding years, although much of these were long past their sell-by date.

Alongside re-roofing, a few minor alterations to the roof over the south wing, South Tower, and part of the western roof slope were proposed. These works included adjusting and adapting the existing configuration to improve layout and shedding of water. Chimney stacks were repaired and rendered where necessary, and flues leading to the principal rooms were relined so that fireplaces could be used.

It was agreed to cover the area of the south wing and South Tower with a scaffold roof so that works could carry on underneath and be protected from bad weather. This was the one time we used a roof cover, as it was too expensive to contemplate using it again for the main house. We purchased the scaffold quite early on with the view that we could sell it for a profit when the job was finished. This allowed us to move the scaffolding around the house as we progressed with the restoration and freed us from any time-pressure on renting. We are still using it seven years on.

The roof void was occupied by a colony of Greater Horseshoe bats as a summer roost, and in accordance with recommendations from an ecological consultant and the Vincent Wildlife Trust (which had been monitoring the bats for many years), we improved bat access to the roost and to certain parts of the roof void.

opposite Internal roof slopes over the main house, with a roof lantern in front of the huge chimney stacks that link up to the numerous fireplaces in the house.

above Scaffolding covers the entire Phase 1 section of the building, allowing workmen to strip, repair and re-slate the roof.

THE EXTERNAL WALLS

below The proposals to repair the existing brick walls were informed by a series of trials including mortar repair of damaged brickwork, patch repointing and the use of lime render.

opposite Drawing of the north courtyard elevation, showing assessment of the render repairs and the replacement needed. Lost and failing sections of render were renewed and then the entire face was limewashed, coloured with lime putty, raw sienna, and burnt umber.

The external walls are mainly of brickwork, first colour-washed during early phases of construction in the seventeenth century, cement rendered in the early nineteenth century and then exposed following my father's removal of the render in the 1970s. This was one of my father's boldest decisions, and he was determined to return the house to its original brick finish. It turned out to be a masterstroke as the brick has a much softer feel than the cement render and gives the house its character.

Several brick repair trials were conducted in the summer of 2010 by MB Conservation with input from Historic England and the conservation officer, Ray Bird. The approach would form the basis of future repairs to the rest of the house, so it was absolutely crucial to get it right. I felt the worn brick was very much part of the charm of the building and I had a strong preference for a 'light touch' approach to the conservation. Thankfully, there was unanimous agreement.

The scars on the brick of the South Tower were some of the worst on the entire house and therefore formed an excellent testing ground to see the results. Our plans included rebuilding the crenellated parapet (which was part of my father's original vision), where the tower had been chopped off and now only a jagged line of bricks remained. This would reunite the South Tower with the rest of the south wing and would restore the eighteenth-century design to that part of the house.

From the trials, it was felt that it was not possible to design a standard mortar mix to repair the bricks because there was so much variation within the brickwork. Each brick repair would therefore have to be mixed and coloured to match the individual areas. The parapet brickwork had decayed far more than the rest. Here, full flush pointing of the brickwork was used and 'penny-struck' (a process, popular in the eighteenth century, where a line is cut into the mortar between the bricks) to re-emphasise the shape and shadow lines of the bricks so that they could be seen individually from the ground below.

There was also moulded stone and render detailing to windows, doors and quoins (the embellished exterior

corners of the house). Iron cramps embedded throughout the stonework surrounding the windows needed to be carefully removed because they were eroding and causing damage. New stone was added back in where needed and render reformed and repaired. The doors and windows were a mixture of painted timber and sashes of varying styles and sizes. Repairs on these were also made where necessary. The Grade I listing of the house gave us permission to paint the exterior woodwork with lead paint, which is much more durable than oil-based paint but now banned from domestic use due to its toxicity. The paint had to be specially ordered, with a license approving its use. Looking at the south elevation and the number of windows, I was grateful for this small concession that would save on future maintenance costs.

The 1970s rendered blockwork wall, which had been created to cap the west end of the house where the south wing had been demolished, formed an uncomfortable bond with the rest of the house. The decision was made to limewash this section and carry the limewash around the west courtyard to tie the two sections of the house together. The alternative was to take down the wall completely and re-build in brick, which would have been a huge job, not to mention prohibitively expensive. At the same time, we added several new window openings to break up the austere-looking wall, bringing natural light into the interior.

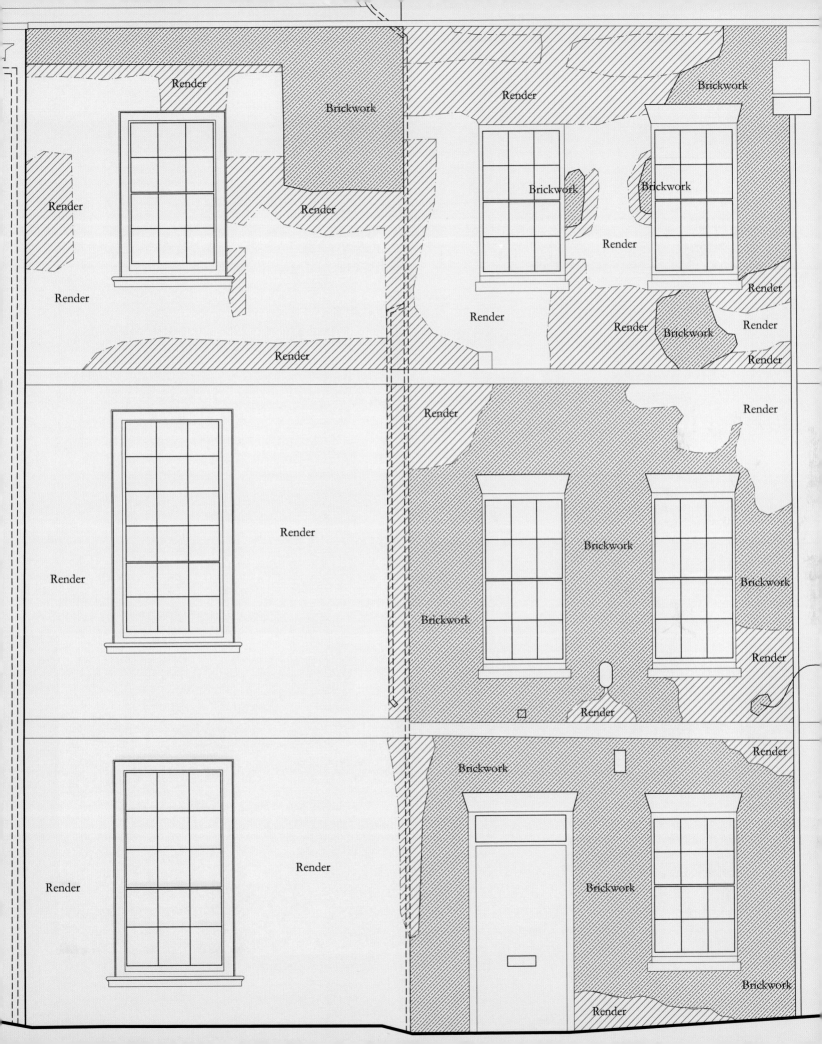

THE FAMILY ROOM

Our Family Room was once my great-grandmother's bedroom and was connected to my father's study through a narrow passageway. During my first visits to the house I vividly remember opening the shutters and hearing them crunch against a large mound of dead flies that had piled up on the windowsill. One of the doors on the west wall opened right onto the 1970s blockwork that had been used to cover the end of the house, where once a corridor led down to other rooms in the demolished south wing. In the middle of the room was a four-poster bed with the family crest embroidered on the headrest. The bed was taken away and carefully restored by Ian Block from A.T. Cronin Workshop and now lives upstairs in our bedroom. The rest of the room was full of dusty boxes and belongings of my great-grandparents including old letters, photographs, riding boots and hat boxes. It felt as if they had simply walked out one day and left everything behind. I spent many hours sorting through the items in this room, pondering their lives.

The walls were decorated with a silver floral wallpaper which we later replaced with a painted Farrow & Ball finish.

This was an approach we implemented in most rooms during Phase 1, except the Green Room and the hallways. A decorative feature of the room was the gilded beads on the door panels and shutters, which were retouched and cleaned by the Humphries & Jones conservation team. This feature was replicated in the Study and Small Dining Room.

below Samples of gilding for retouching the wall and door panel beading. Lynne Humphries of the Humphries & Jones conservation team commented, 'The challenge when restoring existing gilding in a historic property is in the toning applied over new gilding in order to match the appearance of the original. Not too much bling but just enough.'

opposite Door opening under construction. Originally, the doorway led to the south wing, which was demolished as part of the work in the 1970s. A smaller door, which replaced the existing one, now opens to a closet. The larger door was relocated to the newly formed opening leading directly into the kitchen, just visible on the right.

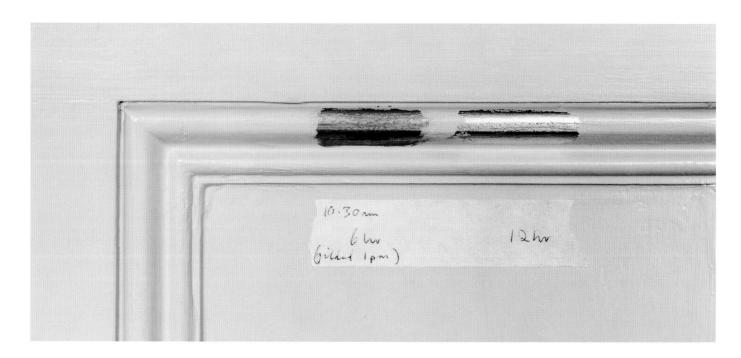

above and right Before and after views of the Family Room, with windows looking south over the lake. The new window seats hide the radiators—and also make a great place for a wandering Bengal cat to perch.

overleaf The family German Wirehaired Pointer, Hettie, acquired from a neighbour, keeping watch over proceedings. The sign on the wall dates from the 1950s when the house was open to the public for a brief period following the Second World War. The current Earl's grand-aunt Lettice supervised the tours.

THE KITCHEN

Adjoining the Family Room is the kitchen. This room was my great-grandmother's bathroom, and other family members recall her incredible bath with a shower hood and steps going down into it (now stored in the stables, waiting to be brought back to life). A corridor separated the two rooms and one of the major alterations during this phase was to remove the corridor and open up the space to create a bigger kitchen and make a new, more direct opening in the wall of the Family Room. We retained the existing curved ceiling above the kitchen to give an indication of the room in its previous form. The alteration has greatly improved the relationship between the two rooms, which are perhaps the most used in our day-to-day lives. The kitchen itself was designed from scratch and made by local cabinetmakers David Mouland Furniture.

above View looking north into the kitchen. An existing opening to the right was blocked, and access was gained via the newly formed opening in the centre. This structural alteration was one of the few granted by Historic England during Phase 1.

right Two tapestry fragments flanking the door to the kitchen, once installed in the Stone Hall, were found in a chest of drawers in the stables. The crown, dated 1786 and bearing the inscription 'Waste Not Want Not', was rescued from the beer cellar and remounted.

A large photographic print of bluebells taken in a wood on the estate by Justin Barton hangs in the kitchen. The windows of this room provided the main access route into the building during Phase 1, because the only other option at that time was a small basement staircase that was too narrow to accommodate most construction materials and furnishings.

THE STUDY

The Study is sandwiched between the Family Room and the Small Dining Room. We opened up an earlier blocked window on the east wall so that you could see out across the park and down the avenue of beeches. In the winter the wind comes whistling through here, which may have been why one of my ancestors blocked it up in the first place. However, the view made it worth the trouble.

The decoration was guided by close friend and our chief interior guru, Edward Hurst. Edward has been integral to the whole project, not just the Study. We had a lot of old prints and photographs that we rescued from various parts of the house and stables. It was his idea to hang them close together and cover all the walls—an effect that I love. I often find myself drifting off in thought, looking at the pictures around the room when I'm supposed to be getting things done.

above A previously blocked window (left) was opened up for views to the east. The freshly plastered and painted Study (right) awaits furniture and paintings.

opposite The view from the present Earl's desk, with a miniature of the 7th Earl's bust by sculptor Matthew Noble and a carved wood elephant the 10th Earl brought from India for the current Earl when he was a child.

overleaf To the left of the south-facing window sits a large bust of the Earl of Belfast, brother of Harriet, 8th Countess of Shaftesbury. The walls are lined with old family photographs, prints and paintings, which are a great source of inspiration for the present Earl and his family.

GOD SAVE THE KING

THE SMALL DINING ROOM

This is one of my favourite rooms in the house. It was the location of our meetings before the restoration work started. There was a large boardroom table in the middle of the room, with an electrical storage heater in one corner and a modern strip light hanging above. Despite the sparse furnishings, the space always had a lovely feel.

The room has a beautiful decorative plaster ceiling and delicate gilded panelling. Much of the work revolved around conserving these decorative elements. We sadly had to part with the partially shredded golden damask curtains at the windows, and have not found a replacement for them yet.

In our plans, the room was originally intended as the drawing room, even though it was used as a breakfast room by my great-grandparents and was always referred to as the Small Dining Room. However, after we moved in we reversed this decision and it is now a dining room again. The light through the south-facing windows makes it a perfect place for breakfast or lunch, and the size makes it equally suited as an intimate space in the evening.

A lot of the furniture used in the room had been stored at the stables. Much of it had been piled up there during the demolition works in the 1970s and was in very poor condition. We had a real journey of discovery looking through everything with Edward Hurst and took his advice on what to get repaired and what to skip over. The beautiful painted secretaire cabinet was sent down to be restored by Steve Thomas in Cornwall, who did a remarkable job, sensitively repairing and retouching missing paintwork and reglazing the cabinet doors. He recorded the restoration work in several photographs, which he left in one of the cabinet draws. Mike Durkee from Castle House Antique Restoration, who over the years restored and repaired countless items for us, brought the architect's table and side cabinet back to life. Knowing the stories behind each individual piece of furniture makes this room that much more satisfying to be in.

The cast iron front panels of the window seats were

above Detail of plasterwork on the ceiling mid-way through conservation by the Humphries & Jones conservation team.

opposite A section of the fireplace surround, which was carefully cleaned and re-gilded. The earl's coronet on the mantelpiece was last worn by the 9th Earl of Shaftesbury, great-grandfather of the current Earl, at the coronation of King George VI and Queen Elizabeth.

made by the Beehive Foundry in London, who used a template from one of our original radiator cases in the hallway. From this, several casts were created, which we have used throughout the house. We had marble slabs cut for the tops, and underneath is where we have hidden our modern radiators. The tops work really well as warm seats (loved by pets). The foundry work took a lot of time to get right, because the design was surprisingly delicate and hard to replicate.

above The painted secretaire cabinet was found in the stables and beautifully restored by Steve Thomas in Cornwall.

right The completed Small Dining Room with restored furniture, all sourced from the house. The two portraits are of the present Earl's grandfather as a child (left) and Mary, 4th Countess of Shaftesbury (right).

GREEN ROOM

opposite The Green Room was used as storage for the large paintings and tapestries that had been left in the house following the demolition work in the 1970s. Sections of wall were stripped back to bare brick for the treatment of dry rot.

below A detail of the green flocked wallpaper that served as source material for the new paper. The design was carved onto blocks, and the new paper was colour-matched to the original.

Before the renovation, the Green Room was the storage room for the large family portraits and tapestries that were left behind in the house, as they were too big to go anywhere else. They had been moved around the house during previous phases of work, having managed to escape the Christie's sales, and ended up being propped up against each other on racks in this room. Some had become quite badly damaged by plaster from collapsing ceilings and by birds that had found their way in to the house.

Early on, I was put in touch with Dominic Chesterman and his brother, Raph, who had followed the family tradition in painting restoration. Initially, I was interested in getting a few of the smaller paintings worked on, so I gave them two to take away. The results were amazing. Over the years, I kept feeding them more and more paintings, some of which had to be relined, some with damaged frames that needed repairing and some that just needed a good clean. No matter what I've thrown at them they've always come back looking renewed, and we have now managed to work our way through the whole collection—something we can't really believe when we think back to the first time we discussed the project in the Green Room. I've always been astounded how well paintings come back to life. I remember vividly the day we reinstalled the two large paintings of the 7th Earl and his wife, Emily, (painted

left Portraits of the 7th Earl and Countess of Shaftesbury flank the marble fireplace, which is topped with a George IV gilt overmantel mirror, made in about 1825, with original, distressed plates of mirrored glass. In the centre of the room is an oak-and-mahogany, late-eighteenth-century, seven-sided rent table from Crichel House, a nearby Georgian country mansion.

overleaf The windows of the Green Room (left) overlook the west courtyard. On the far wall is a portrait of the 9th Earl of Shaftesbury in his peer's robes. In the corner sit a regency pollard oak centre table (right) with a pair of George III mahogany bergères, originally from the Library.

by H. Bird and John Lucas, respectively) in this room, and we all stood back and admired the portraits, which had looked so sad for so many years.

The room itself had been partially damaged by dry rot, and the north-west corner had been stripped back to bare brick and was missing the green flocked wallpaper. There was much debate about what to do with the wallpaper, which was an important piece of historical decoration. I felt it should be replaced, given that so much of it was missing, and Historic England were very keen that we should recreate it if we were going to remove the remaining fragments of the original. This is the path we ended up going down, and Allyson McDermott and her team undertook the work. To do this, new hand-carved blocks from grained fruitwood had to be made to replicate the original pattern. The steps of the process are described by Allyson:

The ground colour is mixed from traditional dry pigments to match the original and applied by hand using circular brushes. Each colour is printed sequentially, each block having first been carefully registered. If flock is to be applied, this is dusted on the surface whilst the ink is still sticky, then the excess shaken off. The flock is hand-dyed and cut from pure wool. Each print is unique, with its own individual characteristics and a wonderful textural quality which cannot be reproduced by any other means.

The results produced a very vibrant and striking paper that gives the room a lot of character. After going through so much trouble to recreate the wallpaper, it amused us when we later found an even older red paper that had been covered by a picture rail.

It was satisfying to piece together the room once the wallpaper was installed; with the sofa that we had reupholstered separately and the large chairs in a burnt orange velvet, all seemed to sit surprisingly well in the room. We also commissioned two cabinets, with marquetry panelling on the doors, from local cabinetmaker James Winby. One is dedicated to drinks; the other to music, with space for some vinyl and a record player.

THE HALL & LANDING

Other than the hallway linking the rooms in this first phase of work, which was decorated with a neutral white-and-grey striped paper, all the landings and corridors in St Giles House had blue-striped 'silk effect' wallpaper. In some patches this was several layers thick. Over time, dampness and water ingress had caused staining and some of the pattern in the wallpaper had started to run, creating some unique effects. Where this damage was not too extreme the results were pleasing, and later in the project we spent a lot of time preserving the wallpaper, touching it up and cleaning it. It was always something that made an excellent background for photography, which we found out with the various photography shoots that were done at the house. In the end, the blue became somewhat of a St Giles trademark, with Farrow & Ball even naming a paint colour after the house. The hue was also the inspiration for the wallpaper we used to redecorate the downstairs hallway and the first-floor landing.

right The bedroom-floor landing before the ceiling and floor were repaired. All the floors had to be lifted to put in new pipework and electrical wiring. The last time the house had been upgraded was in the early twentieth century. Plumber Nigel Cutler comments, 'Without a doubt it was the most demanding, challenging and stressful job of my life. But it was also the most enjoyable, satisfying and rewarding. It has left me with a huge sense of pride and achievement. Would I do it all again? Too right I would.'

opposite A sneak view into the Stone Hall, where a number of busts wait to find out where they'll end up in the house.

overleaf The blue striped 'silk effect' wallpaper covering the walls of the main staircase was painstakingly conserved by Tim Cant, who observes, 'It is the only job where I have had to work on such a large expanse of wallpaper while repairing so many tiny damaged areas! I was replacing hundreds of small pieces of paper, maybe 5 × 10 mm, into a huge wall of wallpaper.'

above Alexandre Serebriakoff painted a watercolour of the hall by the back staircase in the south wing in about 1949.

right A view of the south wing back staircase today. A new door has been inserted into the wall under the stairs, which provides direct access down to the estate office. The pictures surrounding the oval mirror in the work by Serebriakoff are now hanging along the staircase to the floor above (installed after this photograph was taken). The wall-mounted clock in the watercolour has been relocated to the Study. Unfortunately, the original blue wallpaper was replaced in the 1980s with a grey-white paper; a new Farrow & Ball drag-effect paper was recently installed to reintroduce the blue colour. The original blue of the walls provided the inspiration behind Farrow & Ball's St Giles Blue paint.

THE MARLBOROUGH ROOM & BATHROOM

One feature on the bedroom floor is that all the rooms have names, which are painted above their doorways. The Marlborough Room, named after the 6th Countess who was one of the daughters of George Spencer, 4th Duke of Marlborough, was for a time my grand-aunt Lettice's bedroom. We had decided it would become our master bedroom. It had a unique arched window on its south wall, which had been a later insert and gave the room fantastic light and views across the lake. I remember the first night in the house, lying in bed and listening to the ducks as they woke up at dawn.

An interesting feature of the room was the decorative moulding, made from papier mâché and produced by Bielefeld and Co. sometime in the nineteenth century, which formed rectangular panels on the walls. We wanted to remove a section of this to make way for the bed and to form a new opening in the north wall to provide direct access to the bathroom. We had a good deal of back and forth with Historic England over the importance of the moulding and whether removing it was acceptable, but in the end we were able to take some sections down and store them.

The new doorway to the bathroom also provided access to a corridor, which had previously led down to the demolished south wing. Where the blockwork wall had been built, a void existed between the new wall and the end of the old house. This void provided a perfect place to create a small dressing room. The wallpaper we used was a copy of some lovely vine-patterned, hand-printed paper we found hanging in the corridor here.

The Marlborough Room before work commenced, with its distinctive papier-mâché decoration on the walls. The reflection in the mirror shows the dreadful condition of the opposing wall.

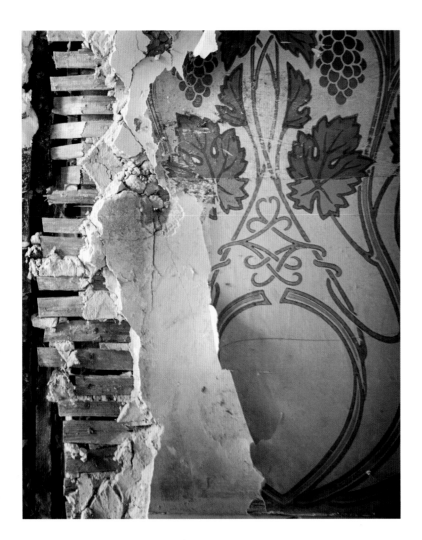

above A fragment of Vine wallpaper produced by Jeffrey and Co. in 1893, which was reproduced and replaced in the corridors leading off the Marlborough Room.

right A four-poster bed with the family crest on the headboard, which was restored and relocated from the Family Room (formerly the bedroom of the 9th Countess). In the centre of the room is an eighteenth-century English needlework carpet, previously from the Stone Hall.

overleaf An arched window looks south across the park.

left A sleeping bust on a window seat.

opposite The restored fireplace surround with a Shaftesbury Bull, a symbol of the Ashley-Cooper family, and a robot sharing the mantelpiece. The family tree of the 3rd Earl of Shaftesbury hangs above.

overleaf The bathroom, with eighteenth-century watercolours depicting views of St Giles and the Park.

THE CECIL ROOM & BATHROOM

The Cecil Room, likely named after the surname of our longstanding neighbours in Cranborne, the Marquesses of Salisbury, was located directly below the site of the demolished South Tower and leaking water had left it in very poor condition. There was a pile of old books and fabric heaped up in the corner of the room, and several sections of ceiling had collapsed. It had a beautiful built-in white-painted wardrobe that was full of old flags.

One door led through to a dressing room, which had been shelved and was used as a linen store. It also contained sets of old china bedpans and washing bowls. Owing to the complication of getting water to upstairs rooms (and typical of an earlier period), there was a lack of bathrooms on the bedchamber floor—only three full bathrooms accommodating numerous bedrooms. In the Cecil Room, the dressing room made a perfect bathroom and had beautiful views looking across the park to the south and east.

below A linen cupboard and china store, full of old quilts, sheets, bedpans and other china for the bedrooms—left completely untouched for years.

opposite The shocking state of the bedroom was due to water penetration as a result of the demolition works in the 1970s. Only a temporary roof covering was keeping the elements at bay.

above The removal of the shelving in the linen cupboard and china store created space for a light-filled bathroom with windows facing east and south.

right The restored guest bedroom with newly acquired brass bed and old Japanese hanging scrolls that were found in the house.

THE HANDEL ROOM
& BATHROOM

opposite Details of the rooms before renovation.

below Some of the original floral wallpaper in one of the cupboards was saved, but otherwise the room was repainted in ochre to liven it up for the family's three children. The circus painting was found in the basement.

overleaf The ochre walls and orange trim were repeated in the bathroom. The photographs over the bathtub are by Paolo Woods.

The 4th Earl of Shaftesbury was a patron of George Frideric Handel, and the composer is known to have visited St Giles, with this room named in his honour. At one stage the house possessed one of the largest private collections of original Handel manuscripts, though these are now held at the Gerald Coke Handel Collection, part of the holdings of the Foundling Museum in London. Music has been a theme in my family stretching back many generations.

The room has now become the children's bedroom. It was completely repainted except in one of the cupboards, where we have retained a section of the original floral wallpaper. The bedroom had been full of books, which were all relocated to the library. The dressing room was converted into a bathroom, and a small jib door acts as a secret passage through to the Southampton Room, another bedroom.

PHASE 2

THE GOAL FOR PHASE 1 WAS TO FINISH BY CHRISTMAS 2011. Anyone who has had a building project with a Christmas deadline knows this is wishful thinking. We still hadn't begun the painting and decorating when Christmas was upon us, and we became resigned to the fact that the project was going to overrun. By this stage, Dinah was pregnant with our second child, Viva, so we were keen to move in before the baby came in April. It dawned on me that we could be living in the house within the fiftieth year of my great-grandfather's death, which had been on 25 March 1961. He was the last inhabitant at St Giles, and this felt like a significant anniversary. I used this as a new target, and in the last month everything came together. We officially spent our first night in the house on 23 March 2012, moving in with two days to spare.

It was a very special moment, which both Dinah and I will always remember. The house welcomed us in with open arms on a sunny day. We felt so excited to be starting a new chapter in its long history and raising a family, who would grow to know it as their home. Not long after we moved in, our daughter Viva was born. Mike Burleigh, who had been working on the house doing emergency repairs in 2002 and who was now helping with the brick repairs on the exterior, told me that the moment he heard children's voices in the house was when it really hit him that the house had returned to life.

However, there was still plenty to do before it felt like a real home. Our bedroom consisted of a mattress on the floor, and we had builders surrounding us day and night. Our excitement about moving in partially distracted us from the near constant noise and dust, which became part of our day-to-day lives, but living there in the early days sometimes felt like an endurance test. By this stage we had decided on further work, and Phase 2 was well underway. Whereas Phase 1 had been about creating a space for us to call home, Phase 2 was intended to make the house viable as a business.

In the pre-renovation Great Dining Room is a ghosted image of a large George II giltwood mirror, which sold at one of the Christie's sales in 1980. The shadow of the mirror was inspiration for the future work on this room.

opposite The servants' staircase leading up to the attic, badly damaged by water penetration, had partially collapsed.

overleaf The attic space was previously subdivided into bedrooms. The partitions were taken out in the 1970s, and it is now one large open space which is currently used to store furniture and items from around the house.

Discussions about a Phase 2 began not long after work on Phase 1 was underway. Two key things happened to trigger this decision. Firstly, we had become more knowledgeable about the house and more experienced in knowing what needed to be done. Now that skilled craftspeople were on site and the project had started, there was an opportunity to capitalise on the momentum. Secondly, we knew it was imperative to start making the house pay for itself. We were inspired by visiting others who were living in historic houses with young families, and saw how life could work, managing a family and running the house as a business at the same time. We began to realise there was a huge opportunity to use St Giles as a venue to generate income. In order to make it a success I knew we needed to press on as far as we could. This was when we really committed everything financially to make the house work, which required significant borrowing. I was convinced that once the house was back together we would be able to pay back the loans.

We needed the principal rooms to be available to host events. This would include creating facilities that would make the house more practical as a venue, such as a lift, lavatories and a commercial kitchen. We also needed the house to look finished from the outside, which would involve tackling the awful scar on the north side left by the demolition of the North Tower. This latter section became a separate phase of work we called Phase 2B.

The danger of not continuing with the work was that we would be stuck in a no-man's-land where we were not able to generate income despite having already invested a considerable sum in the building. Furthermore, there was the worry that the unrestored parts might go on deteriorating or even collapse, creating even more work in the future. In my mind, it was now or never.

The roof over the main house had been a major source of problems over the years. When the roof was remodelled during the nineteenth century, the internal downpipes that took water away from the inner roof slopes were too narrow for the volume of water, and access to them was almost impossible due to the lack of inspection hatches. Two downpipes ran internally down to the basement through a void between the Stone Hall and the Great Dining Room. Over time, water seeped out into the internal walls, and this was a large part of the reason dry rot spread through much of this part of the house. The roof was re-slated and modified to provide better access to the downpipes and also make them larger. All the dormer windows were repaired and repainted. Some of the ones on the south side were so badly decayed they had to be replaced completely.

THE ATTIC

As part of his work in the 1970s my father had intended to remove the nineteenth-century attic floor. The attic space had been divided up into rooms used by the house staff, and my father removed all the internal partitions in this space in preparation for taking off the roof. Thankfully he went no further. However, without the support of the internal partitions the roof was unstable and had started to collapse inwards, and we inserted a steel frame inside the attic for additional support. What remains is a very useful open space that reminds me of an old New York loft apartment. It currently houses my vinyl collection, and we store old furniture there; but in the future I can't help but think the children will take over this space and make it their own.

The external work on Phase 2 followed much the same pattern as in Phase 1, stitching cracks, repairing and repointing the brick where necessary, removing iron cramps, conserving or replacing worn Chilmark stone from around the windows, and touching up render where needed. The one elevation that caused the most difficulty was the south where the removal of the two bay windows had resulted in two orange patches of 1970s brickwork, and simple window openings with crude cement lintels. To unify this side architecturally we added some new stone lintels and rendered the surrounds to the windows to tie them in with the others. We also needed some strategically placed wall climbers to help mask the 1970s brickwork.

DANGER

PLEASE
TAKE CARE
ON
THESE STAIRS

LIBRARY

The Library is one of the most beautiful rooms in the house. It was formed out of three rooms joined together in the nineteenth century, and with six large windows all facing south it gets a lot of light and has always had a feeling of warmth about it. The books give the character and make it feel old and lived in. We paid particular attention, when restoring this room, not to touch any of the paintwork on the bookshelves so that we could retain that sense of history.

Since reorganising the books and getting them back on the shelves, we have been working with a group of volunteers from the National Association of Decorative and Fine Arts Societies (NADFAS), now known as The Arts Society, to digitise and repair the books. The project started in March 2015 and is likely to last several years. I am indebted to the wonderful volunteers who give up their time to do this and it is fantastic that we will eventually repair all the books and have a digital catalogue of the whole library.

The bulk of the restoration work was in repairing the south wall where one of the Victorian bay windows had been removed. This involved reforming the wall cornice and window surrounds, against a combination of bare brick and 1970s blockwork. When we started, two of the bookshelves were propped up against the brick wall and you could see through gaps to the outside. Plastering this wall and fixing the bookshelves made a huge difference to the feeling of the space.

We also added new red mohair velvet fabric to the walls, which replaced a previous red fabric that was too tired to

right, top The Library, as furnished in the 1890s, with one of the bay windows that was later removed in the 1970s demolition visible on the left.

right, middle and bottom The Library in the 1950s—with the addition of two protruding library shelves dividing the space up into three areas—echoes the previous layout of this part of the house, which used to be three separate rooms.

opposite Anthony Ashley-Cooper, 10th Earl of Shaftesbury, in the Library in about 1970, aged 32.

above, opposite and overleaf The Library holds books dating back to the sixteenth century. The oldest collection of books comes from the 3rd Earl of Shaftesbury, an influential philosopher. Anthony Payne, who advised on the conservation and organisation of the Library, commented, 'On my first visit, I must admit that I felt rather overwhelmed by the sheer size of the Library as a room, the ramshackle arrangement of the books and awkward placing of the shelves, some of which had collapsed, and the general feel of gloomy neglect. The environment was cold and draughty, but not damp, and the draughts at least meant that over the years there had been a good circulation of cool fresh air around the books, so I soon realised that although uncared for, the books were actually in not too bad a state and in a relatively favourable environment (for them, if not ideal for human comfort!).'

keep. This new wall covering acts as a backdrop to the gilded picture frames and other antiques such as an eighteenth-century Benjamin Vulliamy longcase clock. The clock was one of the standout finds from our early searches through the stables. Edward Hurst, whose father was passionate about clocks, initially found the case and became very excited, but this was tempered by the fact that it was unlikely that the rest of the clock could have survived. However, after a little more digging we came across a cardboard box, quite separate from the case, that contained the pendulum and the movement. The whole clock was intact and with a little cleaning and coaxing by George and Cornelia de Fossard, it was back, as good as new. Ever since we got this antique working I have marvelled at how well clocks last. There is something beautiful about the simplicity of a pendulum clock in the modern age of computing.

There are three eighteenth-century marble fireplaces in the Library, relating to the three earlier rooms that had been there before, and we made sure we had the flues checked so they could be used. Over the east and north doors are two carved oak panels from the fifteenth century, which are likely from the old manor house that had stood on the property before the 1st Earl started his work on St Giles in the mid-seventeenth century.

opposite George and Cornelia de Fossard restored the Benjamin Vulliamy longcase clock found in the stables, along with its original weights, key and pendulum. A George III carved giltwood Ho-Ho bird perches on a floral spray above.

above A sixteenth-century oak panel, possibly taken from the earlier manor house before the 1st Earl of Shaftesbury started to rebuild St Giles House in the 1650s, has been reset above a doorway.

THE SOUTH DRAWING ROOM

below, clockwise from top left Views of the South Drawing Room in the 1890s, the 1950s and in 1949, shown as a watercolour by Alexandre Serebriakoff. The room was lavishly decorated with a large Axminster carpet and fine eighteenth-century furniture, most of which was sold in 1980 at Christie's.

opposite The fine plaster ceiling dates from the 1670s.

The South Drawing Room contains the most important ceiling in the house. It was built during one of the phases of work under the 1st Earl in the 1670s and is made from very fine plasterwork. The southern end of the ceiling was visibly bowing where one of the bay windows was removed, but thankfully the plasterwork had remained intact. René Rice, who worked on many of our ceilings during the project, undertook the conservation work. It involved clearing out debris from the floor voids above the ceiling (approximately sixty bin bags-worth), repairing decayed support timbers and carefully adding fixings to the ceiling to give it more strength and stability.

The south wall and south end of the floor had to be completely reformed due to the removal of the bay window, which included re-carving the delicate window surrounds and dado rail to match the existing design. The original fireplace had been exchanged in the eighteenth century, possibly during the architect Henry Flitcroft's phase of work (it is thought it may now reside in the Stone Hall), which makes the room the exact reverse of the North Drawing Room, where the

opposite Hanging the new silk damask was a delicate operation. Pierre Vuillemenot, who recently did the job, commented, 'Large rooms are always a challenge. Silk damask requires a lot of tension. You must stretch the fabric to a point where in a year or two, when age and sagging will start, the fabric will remain perfectly stretched. To do the job well is one thing, to make sure it stays good for years is another.'

below View through the South Drawing Room to the North Drawing Room.

overleaf A pair of new giltwood pier-glasses, made by Jonathan Sainsbury Ltd and gilded by Jeremy Rothman Carvers and Gilders to match an original pair sold at Christie's in 1980, hangs between windows on the east wall with views out to the Sunk Garden.

fireplace is from the seventeenth century and the ceiling from the eighteenth.

The walls were furnished with gold striped silk with matching gold curtains and pelmets put up by my great-grandparents, but these were rotten and badly torn. Sadly, much of the original furniture and paintings had been sold at Christie's during the 1980s, but old photographs from *Country Life* magazine show how impressive the room was in its heyday.

We decided we should rehang a wall furnishing, but that we should move away from the late Victorian pattern of my great-grandparents to something earlier. An eighteenth-century damask pattern on a silk and linen fabric from Humphries Weaving in Suffolk was chosen, which we felt was

better suited to the eighteenth-century Flitcroft architecture of the room. Historic England felt this was a good idea, and so we set about sourcing the fabric.

When it came to the art of hanging the silk, we were advised to use Pierre Vuillemenot, a French native living in London, who came to the house with a small team and set up camp in our drawing rooms with a ladder and a sewing machine. It was fascinating to see them work, fixing and stretching the fabric over battens. In just over two weeks both rooms had been finished.

THE NORTH DRAWING ROOM

My father had decorated the North Drawing Room in the 1970s with the idea that my parents might use it once the work on the house was complete. Some of the best family portraits hang here, including the 1st Earl in his Lord Chancellor robes; his father, Sir John Cooper; and the 3rd Earl looking every bit the Philosopher Earl. My father had decorated the walls in dark green baize, which we took down and replaced with the same damask pattern we used in the South Drawing Room but in a different colour, so that the two drawing rooms work together. The plaster ceiling was in relatively good condition and needed minor conservation work and some repainting. Repairs were required to the floor structure. The seventeenth-century fireplace is the standout piece in the room, and lighting the first fire there was a great moment.

opposite The hue of the damask was inspired by the gold-coloured silk that hung previously, and great care was taken to make sure it was not too bright. Jenny Newman, from Humphries Weaving, explains, "The fabric has been designed in a special way to give a distressed appearance to the cloth, which brings a feeling of age whilst the combination of silk and linen provides a subtly textured yet luxurious feel to the room. It was important that there was a feeling of unity flowing between both the North and South drawing rooms and so the same design was chosen throughout."

below At the far end of the room is a portrait of the 1st Earl of Shaftesbury in his Lord Chancellor robes, flanked by portraits of his son and daughter-in-law, the 2nd Earl and Countess of Shaftesbury. On the left-hand side is the 3rd Earl of Shaftesbury (see page 214) and over the fireplace is Sir John Cooper (see page 208), the 1st Earl's father.

THE TAPESTRY ROOM

The early eighteenth-century Flemish tapestries hanging in the Tapestry Room were purchased by the 3rd Earl and are part of a set of four depicting the Triumphs of the Gods from the workshop of Albert Auwercx. When the house was unoccupied they had been stored in the Green Room along with the other large family portraits. They were in fragile condition, and small tears were forming where the weight of the fabric had been pulling against the pins holding them up.

A sculptor friend, Stephen Pettifer from Coade Ltd—who had done restoration work on several sculptures at Wilton House in Salisbury, the country seat of the Earls of Pembroke—put me in touch with textile conservator Laura Bosworth, who had also worked at Wilton House and was based in Swanage in south-eastern Dorset. She came over to investigate the tapestries and took the project on. Before Laura started, the tapestries were sent away to De Wit (Manufacture Royale de Tapisseries) in Belgium for a deep soak and clean. Once they were back and fully revived, Laura started the long process of adding threads and bringing the colour back, often replacing the silk that had long rotten away. She also backed them to make them more stable and added Velcro to attach them evenly to the wall. The results are nothing short of astonishing, and it's wonderful to see them hanging again and looking so vibrant.

The room itself had been affected by dry rot, which had caused the loss of a large section of plaster and panelling in the south-west corner and also a hole in the ceiling, which was propped from below. New door surrounds were created and pediments conserved to bring the room back to its previous state. The door in the north wall is Flitcroft's eighteenth-century entrance, which had been subsequently blocked and was used as a window, but which my father later turned back into a door but left incomplete. We now use it as our entrance into the house for events.

preceding pages A George III mahogany sofa and a pair of arm-chairs from 'The St Giles Suite' of furniture commissioned by the 4th Earl and Countess of Shaftesbury, positioned in front of a tapestry attributed to Victor Janssens and Augustin Coppens, woven in the workshop of Auwercx and depicting the Triumph of Bacchus from the series of the Triumphs of the Gods.

above The restored Tapestry Room was used as a storage area for paintings and other prints in the process of being conserved.

right Both tapestries hanging in their previous locations, after careful conservation and cleaning by Laura Bosworth.

THE STONE HALL

The height of the Stone Hall catches you by surprise when you first enter. Your eyes are drawn up to the decorative ceiling within the lantern that looks down over the room. This ceiling was added by architect Thomas Cundy in the early nineteenth century and roofed over what was then an outside courtyard, which explains the room's striking proportions.

The Stone Hall was once a family living space with paintings lining the walls and an organ where family members gathered to sing. My great-grandfather and grand-aunt Maud were particularly keen singers, and recorded songs to disc, which we still have. My great-grandparents added oak linenfold panelling to the walls around the ground floor and the room briefly changed its name to the Oak Hall, but this panelling was removed following dry rot. By the time I came to the house the walls were bare and the room felt cold.

Dry rot had caused a lot of the north wall to be replaced with modern plasterboard. The decorative ceiling had started to fall down and a temporary scaffold tower had been erected to halt its demise. The paintings that once lined the walls were gone, either sold or relocated.

Our initial plan was to do some repairs to the ceiling and lantern, which seemed to make sense whilst we were working on the roof. We realised that we would not have many opportunities to put a full scaffold tower up inside the house, so we seized on the moment to do it whilst the house was a building site. During this work, we encountered a major structural issue. One of the main beams was decayed and was propped from the beam below which supported the gallery floor on the west side of the room. However, the lower beam was also found to be rotten. Given how compromised both beams were, we were slightly puzzled how the gallery floor and roof above had not collapsed. Without stopping to find out, we stripped the decorative plaster away and inserted a steel beam from underneath—a delicate operation that required more than a few hours of head scratching to come up with a solution.

During this work missing sections of plaster were repaired in lath and plaster. The moisture in the wet plaster triggered some re-growth of dry rot, and the area had to be stripped again. Plasterboard had to be used for further work

above A decorative corbel in the new Stone Hall, designed by the architect Thomas Cundy, who was employed by the 6th Earl of Shaftesbury to cover over the interior court.

opposite The stripped-back Stone Hall halfway through the restoration, showing the vaulted ceiling leading up to a large lantern.

in this area. When it came to choosing a paint, we wanted something that would warm up the space and settled on a terracotta colour, partly inspired by the Flitcroft-designed Pantheon at Stourhead. We created it ourselves mixing Farrow & Ball colours.

During the building work we began to have a few visits from prospective wedding couples looking for a venue in which to get married. At the time, it would have taken a huge leap of faith for anyone to book their wedding with us, given the house was half covered in scaffolding, but we felt we should be getting the word out anyway. On one of the visits, I took a couple, Sally and Pierre, into the Stone Hall and mentioned it would be a great place to hang a disco ball. I saw their eyes light up, and I knew in an instant I was committed to following through on the idea. I'm not sure if that clinched the deal, but either way, they decided to take the plunge and get married at St Giles. They became our first wedding couple, and we will be forever indebted to them for trusting us to deliver for their big day.

right An 1870s view of the Stone Hall with the marble bust of the 7th Earl of Shaftesbury (now in the entrance hall) facing an organ, which was used regularly for entertaining.

overleaf Close-up view of the decorative plasterwork on the inside of the lantern.

above The lantern was possibly inspired by the plans of eminent architect Sir John Soane, who was initially engaged to do work at St Giles House in 1793, before Thomas Cundy took over.

opposite The renovated space has terracotta walls, whose colour helps to give the space warmth, and a disco ball for late-night entertainment.

GREAT DINING ROOM

preceding pages The Great Dining Room in about 1950, looking through into the Tapestry Room. The room was furnished by the 4th Earl of Shaftesbury in the 1740s and designed by the architect Henry Flitcroft. The giltwood chandelier was sold in 1980 and is now owned by Ann and Gordon Getty in San Francisco.

By the time we came to think about the Great Dining Room we had been working on the house for over two years. Initially, I wasn't convinced that we were going to get around to doing it, and could see the house working well as a venue without it. The room had been devastated by dry rot and a huge portion of the panelling had been destroyed. Much of the walls were bare brick, and parts of the room, including the fireplace and overmantel, were in pieces on the floor. The paintings survived, but just barely, after they had been saved from a Christie's auction in the 1980s. They were in the auction catalogue, but in a taxi on the way to the sale my father was persuaded by a friend to withdraw them and save them for the next generation.

However, during the project our approach towards the restoration had evolved. In the early days our focus was on getting rooms back to their original condition as much as possible. As we moved forward, we began to appreciate the unrestored parts just as much. They felt like a unique part of the house and its history. It dawned on us that the Great Dining Room could be the perfect place to leave in its unrestored state. The brick walls revealed the form of the earlier room before the eighteenth-century panelling was created, with old windows and doorways clearly visible. With this exposed, the history of the room could be seen and appreciated.

I approached the Country Houses Foundation (CHF), a charitable grant-giving organisation set up to support the preservation of buildings of historical or architectural significance in England and Wales. Thankfully they embraced the idea and gave a grant to aid a large portion of the work in this room. It is now, without a doubt, the room that most people talk about and the one we are most proud of. I shall always be grateful to the CHF Trustees for their support.

above Looking up through scaffolding at the decorative ceiling, which remained remarkably intact.

opposite Looking west towards the doorway leading to the White Hall. The exposed brick wall and missing sections of panelling are a result of a dry rot outbreak in the 1970s and 1980s.

opposite, clockwise from top left Portrait of Susanna, 4th Countess of Shaftesbury; the partially completed overmantel; the detached overmantel on the floor during restoration; a view of the north doorway leading to the Tapestry Room.

right The marble fireplace and overmantel, after restoration by Mike Burleigh. The portrait shows the sons of the 2nd Earl of Lindsey with a globe.

above Detail of cornice decoration. These gilded heads, probably made by sculptor Peter Scheemakers, appear in the middle of the four walls and all survived. The one on the south wall is one of the few remaining pieces of decoration left on this wall, seen attached to the exposed brick above the overmantel.

right The Great Dining Room as it is today. Norman Hudson, through his role as Chairman of the Country Houses Foundation, helped provide some grant aid for the work here. He commented, 'People find a romanticism in ruins. Far from being yet another restored grand room of which many can be seen at St Giles and elsewhere, its condition adds interest and understanding.'

THE DAIMLER

below and opposite John Vickery from McKenzie Guppy Ltd who worked on the car commented, 'I was asked to help with the recently repatriated Daimler DE36, formally a much loved family member. After some harrowing moments sorting a plethora of issues, I had the pleasure of returning one important part of the puzzle. To watch two more generations of the family climb in and set off on a long awaited trip down the drive was our gift to the ongoing story.'

I knew the family had a Daimler, because there were people on the estate who had been around to see it. It had been my great-grandfather's car, purchased shortly after the war. It was a DE36 Straight-Eight Limousine with a Hooper body. For many years it had stood on blocks in the stables, and sometime in the early 1980s my father decided to sell it. I assumed that was the end of the story.

One day on my way back from Belfast, I was searching the internet when I came across a posting for the sale of 'Lord Shaftesbury's Daimler'. I immediately got in touch with the seller to try and ascertain if it was genuine. The car turned out to be the family car, and it was in Malta where it has been

sitting for the past ten years. It had been through several hands since it left St Giles and appeared to be in reasonable condition.

A long protracted negotiation ensued, and I eventually bought the car. A friend and I decided that the only sensible thing to do would be to drive it home. It made it home in one piece, having crossed Sicily, some of Italy and all of France. It subsequently went to the repair shop where I was told I used up nine lives driving it home as only one of the brakes had been operational in addition to a host of other issues. She is now as good as gold.

PHASE 2B

W E NAMED THE NEXT STAGE OF CONSTRUCTION 2B, because it sounded less weighty than Phase 3 and we were all looking forward to finalising the major parts of the project. The rebuilding of the North Tower, to cover the scar on the north side of St Giles House, was the final component of works on the exterior. Once that was finished, the house was complete from the outside and we could take as long as we needed to finish the rest of the interior. It also brought us two more bedrooms, the North Room and the Southampton Room, and a front entrance. When my father demolished the North Tower, he had intended to use the earlier Flitcroft entrance, which leads into the Tapestry Room. From our perspective this was impractical as it took us straight into the house's principal rooms, which we were now intending to use for events. We would have needed to walk through several rooms before reaching our side of the house.

The design of the new North Tower is inspired by the earlier building that once stood in its place, but the height is now in line with both the parapet on the main house and the newly formed South Tower, rather than extending upwards as architect P.C. Hardwick's original North Tower had done in the nineteenth century. The arched window is one of the additions we inserted above the central arch of the loggia, which mirrors two windows on the south. It was this feature that caused most discussion during the planning application stage, with two of the statutory consultees having differing views on what should go there. The rest of the scheme was supported and in the end the planning application went through without any problem.

Restoration of the White Hall's plasterwork involved identifying old fragments of ceiling and wall decoration, reuniting pieces with damaged areas and patching in missing sections with new material, all fastidiously completed by René Rice. René also drew the coat of arms over the central arched doorway which became the template for a new section of plaster decoration. The wood carving of the archway, door pediments and panel mouldings was done by Charlie Oldham, and the rest of the joinery in the room was done by the team of carpenters from Ellis & Co.

THE NORTH TOWER & LOGGIA

The most satisfying aspect of the tower is the symmetry it brings back to the house when looking from the east. This facade has existed since the seventeenth century, as seen on early maps, and it feels the house is now back in balance.

I was particularly nervous about getting the right choice of bricks, given we would be trying to match new ones with the seventeenth-century bricks of the main house (we needed too many to rely on reclaimed bricks). We found The Bulmer Brick & Tile Company, a brickyard in Suffolk that used traditional wood-fired kilns and a similar type of clay from Reading Beds that we have in the bricks at St Giles. This produced the right colour range, although it required time-consuming sorting and selecting. The size variation in the existing brickwork was matched using bricks of two different sizes. The mortar was then carefully selected from different trials, and the bricklayers were asked to copy the pointing from the old brickwork, which meant forgetting all they had learnt about thick, neat mortar lines. The size variation resulted in a subtle unevenness in the joint line, which very closely resembled the original brickwork. It was a labour– and time-intensive process that was occasionally fraught, but the results made it all worthwhile.

The stone loggia is based entirely on Hardwick's earlier design. We managed to find all the original steps and ball finials, which had been discarded in the bushes close to the house, and we reinstated the original marble plaque of the family crest above the central arch. One section of stone cornice was also found in the bushes but was too heavily weathered to reuse. Otherwise, it was made completely from scratch, out of Portland stone, by a team of Ellis & Co. stonemasons led by Sean Clarke. The original was likely to be made predominantly from brick and render, which is why it may not have survived the demolition. Our friend Stephen Pettifer, from Coade Ltd, made the two panthers that sit on either side of the steps.

Elevations showing the location of the new North Tower and loggia from the east (top) and west (bottom). These additions helped bring symmetry back to the building looking from the east, as well as resolving the scar left by the 1970s demolition work.

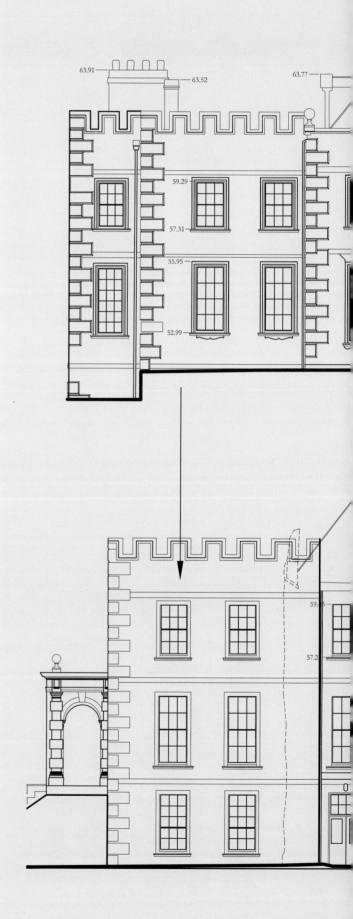

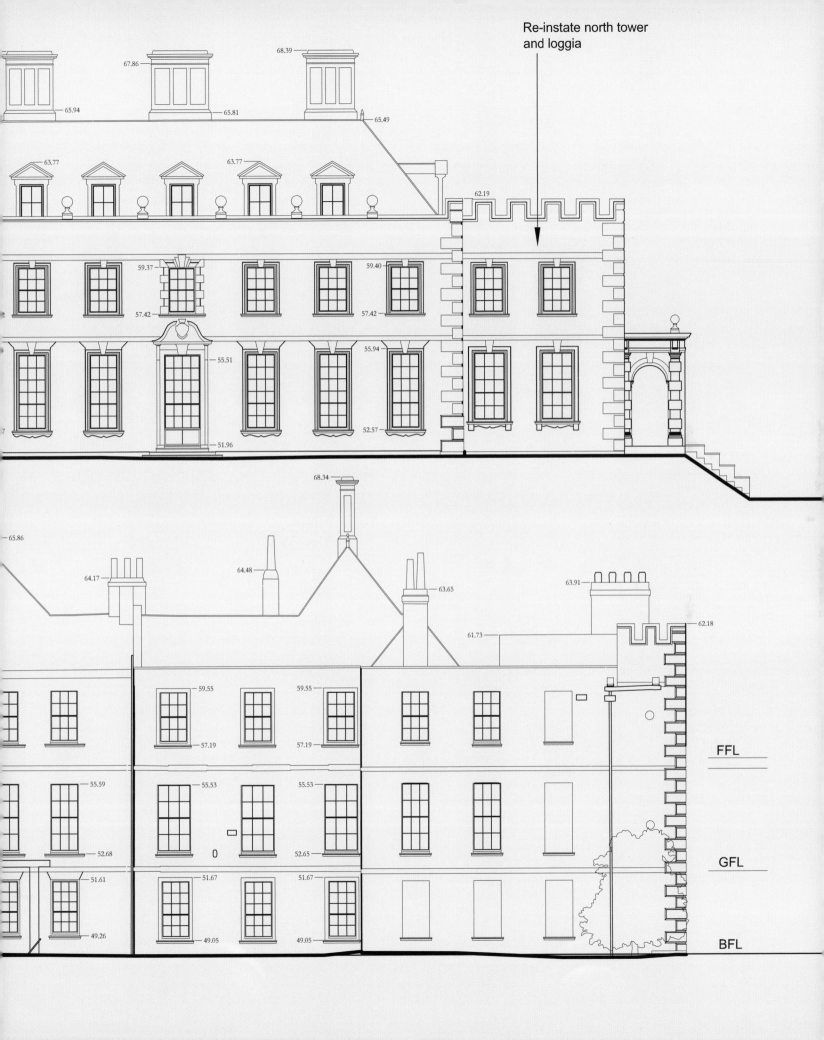

Re-instate north tower
and loggia

67.86
68.39
65.94
65.81
65.49
63.77
63.77
62.19
59.37
59.40
57.42
57.42
55.51
55.94
51.96
52.57

68.34
65.86
64.17
64.48
63.65
63.91
62.18
61.73
59.55
59.55
57.19
57.19
55.59
55.53
55.53
52.68
52.65
51.61
51.67
51.67
49.26
49.05
49.05

FFL

GFL

BFL

below A pile of carved stonework from the old loggia, North Tower and north wing discarded in the trees next to the house. The original steps, ball finials and marble crest were salvaged and reused in the new loggia entrance.

right Riders from the Portman Hunt leading the hounds around the old North Tower entrance and north wing (now demolished).

overleaf Stonemason Sean Clarke, who led the loggia rebuild, wrote, 'The idea that the Tower would be rebuilt wasn't a reality until the drawings were on the desk in the site office. I have been involved with heritage projects all my working life, but I have never built anything quite like the Tower and loggia.'

THE ENTRANCE HALL

For the interior of the tower, we drew on old *Country Life* photographs of the house to restore the architectural design. Some adaptations were necessary in order to add a staircase, which had previously been located in the demolished north wing, and this also enabled us to install a cloakroom opposite. We matched the balustrade and handrail detail from the main stair, which was completed by FRD Ltd. The chequered marble tiled floor was copied from the original entrance hall floor, and partially uses the original tiles, which had been found in a garden shed.

The marble bust of the 7th Earl of Shaftesbury was a present to his wife, Emily, from the Labourers of the Manufacturing Districts of the North of England. My father sold the bust in one of the Christie's sales in 1980, and my cousin Mary Anna Marten bought it, feeling that it should not go outside the family. For years she kept it at her home at Crichel House, a few miles from St Giles. After she died her children decided to donate the bust back to us as they felt it should come home. It was one of the most touching moments during the project, and I am so grateful to them for their generosity. The bust and marble plinth are enormous, and the floor had to be especially strengthened to take the weight.

preceding pages From the loggia, looking east towards the Beech Avenue and south into the entrance hall. The two benches are made from staircase panels dating from around 1660 that have been repurposed as the backs to the benches. They sit either side of the entrance door, in the same location as they were in the old loggia. The lantern is from Jamb.

right The entrance hall with a marble bust of the 7th Earl of Shaftesbury by Matthew Noble. The marble checkered floor is a copy of the original.

The new staircase hallway looking into the White Hall, in construction (above) and completed (right). The handrail and railings of the staircase were created to match those of the house's principal staircase—requiring some intricate woodwork by Oakwrights and metalwork by MJ Patch, Dorothea Restoration and FRD Ltd. The bust is of the 1st Duke of Marlborough, a distant ancestor through the 6th Countess of Shaftesbury.

THE WHITE HALL

The White Hall is one of the finest examples of Flitcroft's work at St Giles. It was also one of the rooms in the worst condition. On the north side, all the panelling had been removed and three huge zinc sheets had been put in place to block the large openings left when the North Tower had been demolished. They rattled in the wind and gave an industrial feel to the building, especially when viewed from the outside. Large sections were missing from the beautiful eighteenth-century decorative ceiling, which was propped up to ensure that it didn't collapse. Much of the panelling on the west wall was also missing, and huge holes gave views from the basement up to the roof.

Our approach here was to try to return the room back to its original form. This involved a lot of skilled conservation and restoration work, including recreating the missing sections of ceiling and plasterwork on the walls, re-carving the wood panelling and door pediments, and refitting the fireplace, which had been moved to Mainsail Haul by my father.

One of the challenges we faced when putting the room back together was that we had no photographic documentation looking north; all of the photographs in the archives looked south, towards the fireplace. We had no way of knowing exactly how the north wall looked. The problem was solved in part by sections of decorative plaster found in the loft of one of the farm buildings and sections of panelling and doors found in another, all clearly from the room. Although the symmetry of the room made some aspects obvious, we had no idea what went above the central doorway leading out towards the entrance hall. In the end, we had to create something from scratch, which was done using the family crest, designed and executed by René Rice.

The 1936 HMV 580 radiogram that sits in the room is my great-grandfather's and was restored by Kevin Minns, who lives in Wimborne St Giles. When I found out he has a passion for fixing old electrical machines, I took him to see the player, which was stored in the stables. He was very enthusiastic and embraced the challenge of bringing it back to life. I was so happy to get the needle on some of my family's old discs that had been gathering dust. The sound you get from the speakers is so warm and teleports one back in time.

above The White Hall ceiling before work started, with some emergency propping holding it together. Dry rot had ravaged the room.

opposite A new door pediment wrapped in polythene and ready to be unveiled, next to panel moulding, all carved by Charlie Oldham. Just visible above the pediment are some of the original plaster fragments found in the stables and carefully re-fixed to the wall, along with new sections of plaster by René Rice.

preceding pages The completed White Hall, with the addition of a George II brass chandelier dating from around 1740 sourced by Edward Hurst.

above The 9th Earl of Shaftesbury's 1936 HMV 580 radiogram, with a record of him singing 'The Gentle Maiden' from *Songs of the Four Nations*, a nineteenth-century collection of songs for the people of England, Scotland, Ireland and Wales. The machine was lovingly restored by Kevin Minns, who said, 'The record-changing mechanism is an engineering masterpiece and seeing it all exposed but gliding through its myriad of super smooth movements for the first time in half a century was a wonderful moment.'

opposite View looking back towards the entrance hall and loggia. All plasterwork and wood carving on the room's north elevation were reconstructed. The two shell-shaped chairs are part of a suite of George II chairs that are original to the house and attributed to William Hallett.

THE JAPAN ROOM & BATHROOM

The Japan Room and Bathroom are located in the north-east corner of the house, the farthest point from any source of water and electrical power. After some careful planning we managed to weave cables and pipework through the house to get to the Japan Room and make it operational. In doing so we have also opened up the rest of the first floor in that section of the house for future restoration projects. It is a beautiful suite and provides the ideal location for brides to get ready when we are hosting weddings downstairs.

The most striking aspect of the bedroom is the chinoiserie wallpaper that we found partly on the walls and partly in heaps on the floor. We decided to take an approach similar to that of the Great Dining Room, carefully cleaning and putting back the surviving sections of wallpaper, and leaving the wall bare in places where pieces were missing. Conservator Tim Cant, who brilliantly worked on the room, recalls,

> *What I remember the most was the day Nick showed me a large room where the floor was covered with scrunched up scraps of paper. There were about thirty pieces in total. Most were large, over 2 metres in length, while others were much smaller, perhaps 10 × 20 cm ... it was a huge jigsaw puzzle. Before they could be rehung, each piece was conserved and cleaned. The surface dirt was removed and any loose backing paper was taken off before tears were supported and each piece was pressed. At the end we stood back with satisfied grins on our faces. A great project to be involved with.*

The bathroom has beautiful seventeenth-century panelling and formed part of the 1st Earl's phase of building work. We sourced the bathroom fittings through Drummonds, partly because of their beautifully designed shower stall, which does not interfere with the panelling.

right The bathroom with fittings from Drummonds which cause minimal disturbance to the seventeenth-century panelling.

THE LANDSCAPE

ST GILES HOUSE SITS PERFECTLY IN ITS LANDSCAPE. I often describe the park that surrounds the house as an oasis. It lies on the south-east edge of the Cranborne Chase and West Wiltshire Area of Outstanding Natural Beauty and is also partly in the Conservation Area of Wimborne St Giles. The 170 hectares is completely enclosed by trees, and stunning views stretch out from the house on all sides. It is easy to admire and be inspired by the beauty of nature. It is also a site that has attracted many visitors over the ages. Just on the edge of the park is Knowlton Church and Earthworks, which Historic England describes as 'one of the great Neolithic and Bronze Age ceremonial complexes in southern England'. The park is registered II* on the Register of Historic Parks and Gardens by English Heritage, for its special historic interest.

Like the house, the landscape has been radically altered over time according to different phases of work. Suzannah Fleming's 'The Garden and Landscape of St Giles House, Wimborne St Giles, Dorset' (2006) expertly covers these phases and goes into detail about the influence my family has had in bringing their ideas to the landscape. The most prominent phase of work came in the eighteenth century, under the stewardship of the 4th Earl and Countess, and saw the introduction of the lake, the terraces around the house, and many parkland buildings, of which only the Grotto, Cave and Castellated Arch (or 'Towers') now survive.

When I came back in 2005, it felt like the park ran right up to the front door. The Sunk Garden, created by my great-grandfather, was overgrown and its walls were crumbling. Nothing remained of the formal planting on the south side leading down to the lake, and the bridges around the lake walk had collapsed. Stretching out to the east the Beech Avenue had all but disappeared, except for a short section of trees by the house replanted by my father following a storm in the

left View of the park and some of the specimen trees at sunset.

overleaf View of the house from the south lawn. Wildflower meadows break up the large areas of lawn surrounding the house.

1990s. The lake was heavily silted and the remaining parkland structures were buried deep beneath the undergrowth. I was resigned to the fact that any progress on bringing the park back to life would be slow going and that it would have to take a back seat to the house.

However, in 2010 the opportunity arose to apply for grant funding through a new Higher Level Stewardship agreement with Natural England, which if successful would help fund the restoration of the key historic elements of the landscape and at the same time safeguard the nature conservation interests of the estate. The application was worked up in consultation with Historic England and Natural England via a Parkland Plan, which was put together by Chris Burnett Associates in May 2010. The Parkland Plan identified all the aspects of the park that make it a special place, including its history, ecology and hydrology. It also provided recommendations on what work should be carried out and provided budget estimates for doing it. The major work identified included: de-silting the lake, restoring the lake bridges, covering over the culvert (which runs under the house and had partially collapsed on the south lawn), restoring the Castellated Arch, restoring the Grotto, stabilising the Pepperpot Lodges and replanting the Beech Avenue.

Given this was following the 2008 economic crash, I was concerned that we would get to the end of the process and find that the funding had dried up. But I was proved wrong, and in August 2011 our plan was accepted and we were awarded £714,500 (84.3%) of grant aid towards implementing the project. It was a huge result. As part of this, 112 hectares of arable land on the estate was also set aside for environmental initiatives.

The house is surrounded by 400 acres of parkland which has been cultivated since the Second World War. Specimen trees dot the landscape.

THE SUNK GARDEN

My great-grandfather, the 9th Earl of Shaftesbury, created the Sunk Garden in 1905. He wrote in his diary:

One of the first improvements we attempted when we came to live at St. Giles's was to dig out the East front and form a Sunk Garden. No architect was employed, we simply followed out the lines of the terrace and steps already there and formed a broad terrace walk which makes the boundary on the East. The whole work carried out by our own men. It turned out a good improvement for it raised the house on that side and made it more imposing the ground being until the ground was dug out, a long flat lawn with a path running down the centre.

I've always felt the Sunk Garden was a great contribution to the house, and it feels like it has always belonged here. Over time it had become wild and overgrown, and so the first task was to bring the structure back, reshaping the paths and forming the borders again. It wasn't until we had diggers undertaking this work that it struck me how large the area is! It must have been a huge job to create it by manpower. We levelled off the four lawns in the centre and added new turf to form an even, easy-to-maintain surface. Jane Hurst chose the plants to go in the borders, and Alison Verrion did the planting. Together they have done us proud.

The icing on the cake was placing in the central pond a cast of a new edition of the statue popularly known as Eros that tops Sir Alfred Gilbert's Shaftesbury Memorial in Piccadilly Circus in London. The figure is actually Anteros, the god of selfless love, and represents the philanthropy of the 7th Earl of Shaftesbury. Gilbert described Anteros as portraying 'reflective and mature love, as opposed to Eros or Cupid, the frivolous tyrant'. The Fine Art Society, which acted as Gilbert's agents for much of his life, published an edition of ten casts in 1985, taken from the original plasters in

An overgrown Sunk Garden looking towards the forlorn Beech Avenue. The paths had been lost, and the walls were crumbling. Many of the ornaments had been taken.

the collection of the Victoria & Albert Museum. These were sold around the world to museums and private collectors, and the figure we acquired was the last one remaining from the edition. The opportunity to bring an important symbol of our family history, and one of the world's most recognisable statues, to St Giles was too good an opportunity to pass up. There is an urban legend that the figure in Piccadilly Circus points to St Giles House. While I have found no evidence to support this claim, I made sure, with a little help from Google, that we have ours pointing back to Piccadilly Circus.

above The Sunk Garden mid-restoration. The North Tower is also under construction on the right.

opposite Anteros, better known as 'Eros', ready to be positioned at the centre of the garden. The lawns and borders are starting to take shape. In the distance, the work on the Beech Avenue is underway.

THE BEECH AVENUE

The Beech Avenue stretches for approximately 1 kilometre from one end to the other. It has been a landscape feature in the park since the early seventeenth century. Maps show it has had at least three incarnations. The rows have always been beech, but the 7th Earl commented in his diary that at one stage 'the sides were three deep, the outer trees being Walnut'. When I was young the avenue was very mature, and a lot of the trees fell down in storms during the 1980s and 1990s. My father replanted about a quarter of the trees at the top section, closest to the house, and the rest were left to their own devices. By the time I came back from New York many more had fallen and the sense of an avenue had completely disappeared. New trees and undergrowth had filled in the centre, and the avenue more resembled a wood. I always wanted to recreate the view, and the Parkland Plan finally gave us the chance to do it. The new avenue took approximately two hundred and eighty trees to create, and Anthony and Viva helped plant the first and the last of these.

Looking up the Beech Avenue in about 1900 with a sundial in front of a gateway over the ha-ha leading into the park, taken just before the Sunk Garden was created.

right, top Looking down on the Beech Avenue before any work was started. The front section of trees was planted after a storm in the 1990s.

right, bottom To create the new avenue, the mature trees are felled and the undergrowth cleared and burnt, along with any tree stumps. Once the ground is levelled off, the new trees are planted.

overleaf The newly finished Beech Avenue with a double line of Beech Trees stretching for an entire kilometre.

GROTTO

below The approach to the Grotto. It sits on top of a water spring that flows into a canal and feeds the lake.

opposite The Grotto in ruinous state. Much of the structure was rotten and the shells and other elements were barely intact.

Of all the projects on the Parkland Plan, the Grotto was the most complicated. Built in the 1750s by John Castles of Marylebone in London, it formed part of the eighteenth-century Pleasure Grounds designed by the 4th Earl and Countess of Shaftesbury and Henry Flitcroft. It is listed Grade II*, and the core building has two main chambers. The entrance chamber is encrusted with minerals, flints and crystals and has a patterned pebble floor. The inner chamber is covered with shells brought across the Atlantic from the Caribbean. Large conch shells are hung on hooks and shell-covered box structures and branches create organic shapes that protrude out into the main chamber, giving the Grotto the feeling of being inside a coral reef.

Keeping the delicate structure from falling apart has long been a conundrum for my family, and Philip Hughes, who oversaw its restoration, said it was probably the most challenging project he had worked on. He has a huge folder containing the specification documents to prove it. The main repairs commenced in 2013 and were undertaken by Sally Strachey Historic Conservation.

Over time, large sections of the decorations to the inner chamber had fallen and many of the branches had decayed to such an extent that they crumbled on touch. The floor of the chamber, covered in a thick layer of fallen shells and other decoration, was divided up into a grid pattern, and locations of artefacts were recorded within the grid in an attempt to locate areas from which they may have fallen. The shells were then cleaned and identifiable elements were put back in their original positions.

Large root systems from trees and ivy had to be removed from the structure, which necessitated some partial dismantling and rebuilding of walls. Following this process, intricate consolidation repairs were carried out to structural elements of the chambers, which included the injection of Paraloid resins into severely decayed 'branches' and 'boxes' to strengthen and reinforce them. Areas of decoration surviving in situ were supported from the back (after the roof was lifted to provide access), and key areas of missing decoration were reinstated using photographs and physical evidence. The works were completed in the summer of 2014.

above Details showing the wide range of shells that cover the walls inside the Grotto. Anna Hughes, who was in charge of sorting through the shells that had fallen to the floor, remembers, 'The work was unlike anything else I have been asked to do! I needed to be methodical and careful—the shells and other elements of the fabric were extremely fragile. I spent many (happy) hours alone washing, dusting, identifying and bagging up the shells for their later reinstatement.'

opposite The central chamber of the Grotto with a restored fireplace in the centre of the wall and window openings just visible behind the decoration. A section of the wall had collapsed, and this was painstakingly restored using archival photography as a reference.

THE LAKE, CULVERT & BRIDGES

The lake was created as a 'serpentine river' in 1732 as part of the 4th Earl and Countess's Pleasure Grounds. It is an area abundant with wildlife. Water is carried into the lake by a culvert that runs from the River Allen, and directly underneath the house. At the other end of the lake the water is fed back into the river. The section of the culvert south of the house collapsed in the 1990s, exposing the water channel underneath the south lawn and posing a hazard.

The lake is only a few metres deep in places and therefore it frequently silted up. By the time we started work there was only a few centimetres of depth at the end nearest the house. The last de-silting operation had been carried out in the 1960s, and we were keen to come up with a solution that could solve things in the long term.

As part of the Parkland Plan a comprehensive overhaul of the park's hydrological system was carried out. This was led by Penny Anderson Associates Ltd, working with project manager and landscape consultant Chris Burnett and specialist landscape contractor Will Bond. It included the restoration of the culvert, the installation of silt traps in the lake's feeder stream and a sophisticated telemetric system of flood control. A section of the River Allen within the park was restored, with the aim of reducing flood risk to the park.

To de-silt the lake, the team set up a pontoon system of floating pumps, excavators and conveyors that took the silt away to an adjacent field. Whilst the lake was drained we were able to lay the pipes for the ground-source heating system.

The New Thames Bridge at the northern end of the lake, closest to the house, and the Cascade Bridge at the southern end of the lake were repaired, thus reinstating the walking route around the lake which had been lost for many years. Both bridges had been built by my great-grandfather, the 9th Earl of Shaftesbury.

The New Thames Bridge that crosses the canal leading to the lake in front of the south side of St Giles House. This collapsed and was later repaired as part of the Parkland Plan.

left The lake drained of water to allow dredging to take place. The silt that had built up was removed via conveyor belts and carried to an adjacent field.

top Preparing the culvert to be covered over. The culvert runs under the house and feeds the lake, carrying water from the River Allen.

above View of the freshly dredged lake from the roof of St Giles House.

overleaf Looking back over the lake as the sunlight catches the south side of St Giles House.

CASTELLATED ARCH

The Castellated Arch, sometimes known as the Arch and Towers, is a folly, built in 1748. The inspiration for the building is believed to have come from a large landscape painting by Salvator Rosa that hung in the house. Suzannah Fleming describes its access via a serpentine path in a 'dense evergreen plantation, originating quite near the house' and as the starting point for the Pleasure Grounds circuit. From it, one used to be able to look across the lake to see the 'Castle on the Lake' and also hear the cascade of the River Allen close by, still audible today. From here you would walk to other delights of the Pleasure Grounds, dotted around the lake, such as Arethusa's Temple, the large Chinese Bridge and thatched house, the Pavilion on the Mount, a hermitage, a root-house and rootery, Shakespeare's House, Thomson's Seat (named after the poet James Thomson), a naturalistic flint archway, the Stone Cave and the Grotto. Almost all these structures have now been lost, except for the Grotto, Castellated Arch and Cave which are made of brick or stone and therefore have proved more durable.

S T GILES HOUSE IS AN ANCIENT, HISTORIED PLACE, located in the parish of Wimborne St Giles on the south side of Cranborne Chase in Dorset. According to John Hutchins, in the *History and Antiquities of the County of Dorset* (1774), the Ashley family came to the manor of Wimborne St Giles, then called St Giles Upwymbourne, in the mid-fifteenth century. Originally from Ashley in Wiltshire, where they were lords of the manor, the Ashleys acquired the estate that had been owned successively by the Malmaines, the de Plecys and the Hamelys, through the marriage of Robert Ashley to Edigia, daughter of Sir John Hamely. Their son Edmund Ashley lived here for the first quarter of the fifteenth century, and the antiquary John Leland, who passed through the area around 1538, noted 'S Giles Winburne, wher Mr [Henry] Asscheley hath his maner place and park'—suggesting that it was a house of some degree. A mid-fifteenth-century carved stone armorial plaque, reset into the wall of the Servants Hall (now the Estate Office) in the basement of the present house, may also attest to a building with some pretentions to grandeur. It commemorates the marriage of one John Ashley to Edith Talbot, and is flanked by Talbot hounds, but may have been brought in from elsewhere. Likewise, an undated mid-sixteenth-century inventory describes 'the parler' being richly furnished with a 'chaire' of 'murry velvet imbroidered with white satten', two black velvet chairs, 'a carpet of turkey work' and a screen of 'satten of Bridge' [Bruges]. If this is an inventory for St Giles House, it was already richly furnished for the period.

But it is Sir Anthony Ashley (d. 1628), clerk to the Privy Council, Member of Parliament for Tavistock (1588) and Old Sarum (1593), knighted for his part in the taking of Cadiz in 1596 during the Anglo-Spanish war, who is the first of the family to leave a more tangible imprint on Wimborne St Giles. Sir Anthony resigned his public offices in around 1610, having earlier purchased the house and estates of his cousin Sir Henry Ashley, who had fallen into financial difficulties.

A collection of hatboxes belonging to the 9th Earl of Shaftesbury.

below A mid-fifteenth-century carved stone armorial plaque commemorating the marriage of John Ashley to Edith Talbot, flanked by Talbot hounds. Underneath, twelve rules found in the study of King Charles I.

opposite A detail of the grounds surrounding St Giles House from a 1672 map, showing the east front of the house, recently completed by the 1st Earl of Shaftesbury. The Riding House and adjoining farm buildings are seen to the north (towards the bottom of the map).

In 1620, he entertained James I's favourite, George Villiers,
Marquess of Buckingham, at St Giles and evidently hoped
for a visit from the king himself. This never came about, but
James I sold him a baronetcy in 1622. It was Sir Anthony who
built, in 1624, 'a rank of convenient almshouses', described
by Hutchins as consisting of 'several apartments for eleven
poor people built of brick and the doors and windows faced
in freestone', which still survive next to the parish church.
His activities in the house are less clear, although William
Palmer's survey of 1659 shows a substantial complex of red
brick buildings straddling a stream, probably a branch of the
River Allen—an arrangement that probably gave rise to the
old family story that the original house was moated. The main
house was connected to its outbuildings on the other side of
the stream by a bridge.

What does survive more or less intact today is Sir
Anthony's new 'Riding House and Stables', a substantial red
brick range of buildings which lies to the north of the house.
With its high gables and mullioned windows, it probably gives
us a good idea of the external appearance of St Giles House
itself at this time. Sir Anthony died on 13 January 1628, and
is commemorated in the Lady Chapel of the Church at Wimborne St Giles by what must be his last architectural project, a
handsome, canopied tomb enshrining effigies of Sir Anthony
and his wife, Jane. Sir Anthony's other great memorial is
more prosaic—he is said to have been remarkably successful
in the cultivation of 'Cabbages out of Holland'.

Sir Anthony's daughter and sole heiress, Anne (who
is depicted as a mourner on the tomb), married Sir John
Cooper, 1st Baronet, of Rockbourne, Hampshire, in 1622.
Their only son, Anthony Ashley-Cooper (1621–1683)—the
first to couple the names of Ashley and Cooper—was born at
Wimborne St Giles, although he moved away after the death
of his mother in 1628 and became a ward of court after the
death of his father in 1631. When he finally came into his
inheritance it was much reduced, although it still included
substantial estates in Wiltshire, Somerset and Dorset and a
property called the Black Bull in Holborn in London. 'Saga-
cious, bold and turbulent of wit', Sir Anthony Ashley-Cooper

below Portrait by Cornelius Johnson of Sir John Cooper (d. 1631), Baron of Rockbourne and father of the 1st Earl of Shaftesbury.

opposite Portrait by Sir Godfrey Kneller of Anthony, 1st Earl of Shaftesbury (1621–1683), in armour.

was educated at Exeter College in Oxford and read Law at Lincoln's Inn in London. He later became a Member of Parliament, at first supporting the royalist faction in the English Civil War, having married Margaret Coventry, daughter of Charles I's Lord Keeper of the Great Seal. He travelled widely in his legal capacity on the assizes court circuit, but by 1643 Sir Anthony's diary records him spending more and more time at 'his house at St Giles Wimborne'. In 1644 he abruptly switched allegiance to the Parliamentarian cause, complaining that the King's policies were 'destructive to religion and to the State'. In August that year, raised to the rank of Field Marshal General and leading a force of two thousand men, he besieged and captured the recalcitrant Royalist town of Wareham. Loaded with honours by a grateful Parliament, he went on to attack Sir John Strangeway's house at Abbotsbury, where he tried to burn the defenders alive, causing such alarm that the towns of Sturminster Newton and Shaftesbury surrendered without putting up a fight. Having successfully quelled opposition to Parliament in Dorset, on 19 March 1650 he solemnly recorded in his diary, 'I laid the first stone of my house at St Giles'. This was doubtless in anticipation of his second marriage—Margaret had died in July the previous

year—to Francis Cecil, daughter of the 3rd Earl of Exeter, five weeks later.

The new house was in fact an addition to the east end of the existing manor house, which involved demolishing parts of the old courtyard house in order to do so. The new building comprised a symmetrical seven-bay block looking east, with two short wings behind, connecting it to the earlier fabric. It was considerably loftier than the old range of buildings, having a raised basement, reception rooms on the principal floor, a chamber floor and an attic lit by dormer windows emerging from the hipped roof. The austere new facade, entirely of brick save for a central stone doorcase, was loosely based on a 1638 design by Inigo Jones for a five-bay house for Lord Maltravers. The architect is not known, but comparison with known work by the amateur architect Captain Richard Ryder—who repaired nearby Cranborne Manor and added a wing to that house in 1647–50—is convincing. Cranborne is only two miles away from St Giles House, and its owner, William Cecil, 2nd Earl of Salisbury, was both a neighbour and a kinsman of Ashley's new wife. The new front looked out upon a grand avenue that led the eye towards the eastern boundary of the park. But if the exterior of the new wing of St Giles House was deliberately sober—as behoved a senior commander in the Parliamentary army—the interior appears to have been richly decorated and surprisingly sophisticated. One of the most elaborate surviving features is the plasterwork ceiling of the South Drawing Room, compartmented by finely modelled wreaths of leaves, fruit and flowers, which follows an Inigo Jones design. Another survival is the imposing stone chimney piece in the North Drawing Room, which, with its heavy festoons, lion masks and swags, is close to an Inigo Jones design illustrated much later in John Vardy's *Some Designs of Mr Inigo Jones and Mr Wm. Kent* (1744). Another plainer, stone chimney piece, its frieze draped with a single festoon, now in the Stone Hall, may comprise parts of a chimneypiece that originally decorated the South Drawing Room. The four rooms on the raised ground floor of the new building formed part of a suite of state rooms—grand rooms designed for entertaining the king or other important

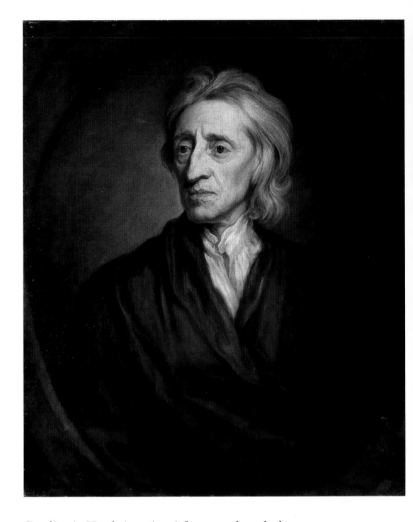

personages—accessed from the much older Great Dining Room. They comprised an anteroom (now the Tapestry Room), a withdrawing room (North Drawing Room), state bedchamber (South Drawing Room) and a cabinet (now the east end of the Library). The creation of a state apartment is considered unusual for a large gentry house at this time—it was built at the height of the Commonwealth.

Apart from a surviving ceiling and the chimney pieces, little is known about how the rooms were originally decorated. However, a much later inventory, of 28 November 1699, suggests that they were always luxuriously furnished. The Great Drawing Room (North Drawing Room) was hung with '2 pieces of Hero and Leander hangings [probably part of a set of the famous Mortlake tapestries illustrating that mythological story] a large looking glass with stands and table to it and a chimney', while the 'Wroat Room' (Bedchamber and present South Drawing Room) was fitted up with a bed and three more pieces of the Hero and Leander hangings.

Sir Anthony gradually grew disillusioned with Cromwell's arbitrary rule, resigning from the Council of State in protest. After the Protector's death in 1658, he was one of the twelve men deputed by the House of Commons to travel to Breda to invite Charles II to return to England. This led to his being created Baron Ashley of Wimborne St Giles by the restored Charles II in the coronation honours of 1661, and he was made a member of the Privy Council. Indeed, Charles II is recorded as staying at St Giles at least once in September 1665, and there may have been further visits. The King would have been lodged in the new Great Apartment. After the fall of his enemy Lord Clarendon in 1667, the new Lord Ashley became a prominent member of the powerful circle of courtiers known as the Cabal (said to be named after the initial letters of Clifford, Arlington, Buckingham, Ashley and Lauderdale—the five lords who formed it). This new influence was accompanied by a rising financial prosperity, as Lord Ashley augmented the income from his estates in Dorset and Wiltshire with foreign speculations. As early as 1646 he had owned a share in a plantation in Barbados, while in 1663 he was appointed by Royal Charter one of the eight Lords Proprietor of the Province of

Carolina in North America. A few years later he became a substantial stockbroker in the Hudson's Bay Company. He was a member of the Royal Adventurers Company from 1663, and, from 1672—when he was appointed by Charles II as the First Lord of Trade and Plantations—its successor body, the Royal Africa Company, a chartered organisation which attempted to gain a monopoly over the English slave trade. It was probably the success of these enterprises, as well as the prospect of further royal favour, that encouraged Ashley to embark upon further alterations to the house in around 1672, the year in which he was created 1st Earl of Shaftesbury and Lord High Chancellor. This was the addition of a new substantial south wing to the house, at right angles to the Great Apartment. Although slightly lower in height than the 1650s iteration of the building, it too was fitted up with a suite of rooms that constitutes a second state apartment. The wing was probably designed by William Taylor, a mysterious London architect who has recently been identified as the author of a number of country houses in the West Country and the West Midlands, many of whose owners had political connections with Lord Shaftesbury. The works at St Giles House were complete by 1672 and are depicted in a survey taken of the park in that year.

The new state apartment on the raised ground floor of the new range incorporated the Cabinet of the earlier, 1650s state apartment, which appears to have been used as a Small Dining Room. A door and a flight of steps led down to the garden. This is corroborated by family tradition; the 7th Earl recalled, 'I have heard my father say that the Lord and Lady Shaftesbury of the time liked to dine early during the summer in the E. room, & then go and play bowls on the Lawn'. This external door also allowed the new state apartment to be self-contained—an important feature when entertaining the very grandest visitors. The Ante-room led to a Great Parlour, a large room occupying much of the middle section of the present Library which could be used as a bedchamber during state visits. The rooms were expensively fitted up—a bill of 5 March 1671 from the statuary William Stanton enumerates 'a sporbled marble chimneypiece with a foot panel £15'. However, the gilded acanthus-leaf cornice in the Ante-room is probably the sole survivor of these luxurious decorative schemes. Downstairs, however, and on the bedchamber floor above, economy prevailed and materials from the old house—floorboards, timber partitions and even windows—were salvaged and reused, although in the basement 'bathing room', under what is now the east end of the Library, a row of rusticated niches suggests the room had some architectural character.

The other major alteration to the house made in the 1670s was the creation of a 'Great Stayre' between the wings of the 1650s block, described in a memorandum of 1670–74 as having 'Hansume rails and Bannisters'. Also designed by the architect William Taylor, it was evidently intended to connect the main entrance to the house, the old ground floor Hall—which in 1699 was known as the 'Stags Head hall' and equipped with '25 stag heads'—with the two suites of state rooms on the main floor. By 1713, the staircase was hung with full-length family portraits, and it may have been the intention to light it from above by a cupola, as in other fashionable country houses of the period, such as Melton Constable Hall,

Norfolk, Coleshill House, Berkshire and Kingston Hall (Kingston Lacy) in Dorset, although it is unlikely that any such feature was ever realised. The staircase itself was destroyed when the Stone Hall was constructed in the early nineteenth century. The 1670–74 memorandum also refers to extensive works in the gardens, constructing walls and gate piers of bricks, burrs and flints, coped with brick and stone, eight feet high around the entrance court, while there were further, even higher, garden walls to the south and east, as well as an iron gate flanked by stone piers with ball finials. The 'bricks, batts and burrs' used in the construction of the walls were taken from the old house—another instance of Carolean economy. The 1st Earl was a keen improver of the gardens at St Giles House; in 1670 he erected a 'Winter-green House' in the old orchard, and his 'Gardening Book', dated between 1674 and 1682, lists thousands of varieties of fruit trees and grafts planted in the various walled gardens.

While these improvements were being carried out, Shaftesbury's prosperity was checked by the pro-Catholic tendency of the royal court. Owing to his intrigues with the Duke of Monmouth to prevent the succession of the King's brother, the Catholic Duke of York (later James II), he was dismissed from the Privy Council in 1674 and ordered to leave London. Retiring to St Giles House, Shaftesbury continued to agitate against the Duke of York's succession to the throne, which resulted in his being confined for over a year in the Tower in 1677. Reinstated on the Privy Council, in 1681 he was again arrested, this time for high treason, supposedly for plotting the death of Charles II. Acquitted and freed in 1682, he fled to Amsterdam where he died in January the following year. He is buried in St Giles Church at Wimborne St Giles. Brilliant, high-minded and quarrelsome, the 1st Earl of Shaftesbury was a controversial figure who has sometimes been claimed as the founding father of the Whig tradition in politics. Certainly his sturdy political independence and views on liberty, rights and constitutionalism made him something of a hero to Whig politicians of the next century, a political philosophy reflected in the influential publications of his private secretary, adviser and friend John Locke.

The 1st Earl's son, Anthony Ashley-Cooper (1652–1699), who succeeded as the 2nd Earl in 1683, was supposedly of 'feeble constitution and understanding'. Derided as 'that unfeather'd two-legg'd thing' by John Dryden in his satirical poem *Absolom and Achitophel*, he certainly suffered from poor health, but this was a cruel jibe rather than an accurate portrait of the 1st Earl's son and heir. Whatever his infirmities, the 2nd Earl made an advantageous marriage to Dorothy Manners, daughter of the 8th Earl of Rutland, who bore him three sons and four daughters. The match was reputedly brokered by John Locke, who later acted as tutor to their eldest son, later the 3rd Earl, with brilliant results. But what is certain is that the 2nd Earl inherited little of his father's energy, and lived quietly at St Giles House for thirteen years, carrying out no major works to the place, as far as it is known.

On his death in 1699, St Giles House was inherited by his eldest son, Anthony Ashley-Cooper, the 3rd Earl of Shaftesbury (1671–1713) who is still remembered today as a moral philosopher, and whose writings were enormously influential in Britain, France and Germany in the eighteenth century. Like his father, he suffered from ill health, but his youthful studies under John Locke and an extensive tour of Europe gave him an exceptionally comprehensive education. Indeed, he only returned to England following the Glorious Revolution and the flight of his grandfather's adversary James II in 1688. Entering Parliament in 1695, where he briefly represented Poole, 'he had the opportunity of expressing the spirit of liberty which he maintained to the end of his life, and by which he always directed his public conduct', by bringing the Treason Act before the House of Lords—doubtless to atone for the imprisonment and disgrace of his grandfather, the 1st Earl. However, chronic asthma cut short his promising political career and obliged him to seek a more salubrious climate abroad. He moved first to Holland, where he mixed in the company of 'several learned and ingenious men', such as Jean Le Clerc, Pierre Coste and Pierre Bayle, who had a great influence on his writings. It was there, among 'liberty loving spirits', that he began to publish letters and pamphlets on diverse ethical, religious and aesthetic subjects. In 1699, he

returned to England on inheriting the Shaftesbury title and estates, which entitled him to sit in the House of Lords, but his worsening health prevented him from taking much part in politics. He turned down the offer of the post of Secretary of State by William III for this reason, and, like many other 'Williamite Whigs', Lord Shaftesbury retired to his estates on the accession of Queen Anne. To everyone's surprise he took a wife in 1709, Jane Ewer, who bore him a son, and it proved to be a most successful union. But once again his delicate constitution, as well as a dread of living beyond his means, drove him again to live abroad in 1703, at first in Holland, and then to Naples in 1711. It was in that year that saw the publication of the first edition of his collected writings on moral philosophy, entitled *Characteristicks of Men, Manners, Opinions, Times*. The 'Philosopher Earl' died in Naples in 1713 of consumption, aged only 42—'with perfect cheerfulness and the same sweetness of temper he always enjoyed when in the most perfect health'. The Earl's body was brought back to Wimborne St Giles by sea for burial beneath a monument adorned with a figure of '*Polite* Literature mourning her most distinguished votary'.

But fame only came to the 3rd Earl posthumously, with the publication of the second, much augmented and revised, edition of *Characteristicks* in 1714. The book became an immediate bestseller, the second most widely read publication in the entire eighteenth century, running into eleven editions by 1790—a statistic only surpassed by his old tutor John Locke's *Essay Concerning Human Understanding*, which achieved nineteen editions in the same period. This secured for Shaftesbury lasting fame as the Philosopher of the Whig Enlightenment—appropriately enough, as he was the first to use the metaphor of light as an allusion to what we now call the Age of Enlightenment.

While living in Naples, in 1712 Shaftesbury finally finished *A Letter Concerning the Art, or Science of Design*, which became a highly influential manifesto on good taste. The essay was widely circulated in England, although it was not actually published in full until 1732. In it Shaftesbury advocated sobriety and simplicity in both architecture and

ANTHONY EARL of SHAFTESBURY 16 84

SIR PETER LELY

opposite Portrait by John Closterman of Anthony, 3rd Earl of Shaftesbury (1671–1713).

below The Philosopher's Tower, built by the 3rd Earl of Shaftesbury around 1707 as a quiet, reflective space. The retreat is situated on the highest point of the old deer park and was visible from the Library windows, then on the east front of the house.

garden design, and the rejection of the sort of 'counterfeit ... Magnificence' typified by Blenheim Palace and the parterres of Versailles. But the 3rd Earl's long absences abroad meant he had little opportunity to practise what he preached—a new back stair, a chimney piece in the Avenue Room on the principal floor of the house, which once formed part of his famous library, and some panelling—are all that can be attributed to his reign at his beloved St Giles House. Of the gardens, he wrote to his sister Elizabeth in April 1706 that he was 'mightily buisy in planting and other such Work', noting that the improvements 'answered as well or better, to Convenience and Health than Ornament'. He also wrote of planting 'great Oaks in a line that guides ye eye from ye Design'd Summerhouse'. This was probably the simple, square brick tower with a domed, tiled roof that was built on an eminence in the park to the east of the house. Now called The Philosopher's Tower, it is the principal memorial of the 3rd Earl at St Giles House.

The 3rd Earl's eldest son, Anthony Ashley-Cooper, the 4th Earl of Shaftesbury (1710–1771), inherited in 1713 when he was only three years old. Brought up in England by his godfather and guardian, Lord Halifax, and tutored by Pierre Coste, he became an intelligent and cultured young man, who revered his father—commissioning a new, revised edition of his *Characteristicks*—and encouraged the scholar Benjamin Martyn to embark upon writing the 3rd Earl's biography. Despite his father's perpetual concern about money, the 4th Earl came into a substantial inheritance, augmented by the proceeds of the sale of the family share in the Carolina Colony to the Crown in 1729 for a reported £50,000. He found a good match in his first wife, Susanna Noel, the daughter of the 3rd Earl of Gainsborough, whom he married in 1725. The new Lord and Lady Shaftesbury were prominent members of the circle of Frederick, Prince of Wales, son of George II, championing the English oratorios of George Frideric Handel over imported Italian operas and patronising the satirical anti-establishment playwright John Gay. Indeed, Handel became a friend of the couple, as did the poet James Thomson. Lady Shaftesbury was also an early patron of the cabinetmaker Thomas Chippendale. Known in the family as 'the great Decorator of the

place', 'Countess Susan' made many improvements to St Giles House. The accounts for building works in the years 1732–50 survive, at least in part, and give a good idea of the transformation of the house, garden and wider estate at St Giles House under her direction. Indeed, the sheer amount of building activity on the estate called for 'extraordinary disbursements' in 1737. An early project appears to be the rebuilding of the old parish church of Saint Giles at the gates of the park, which was supervised from 1732 by George Osboldestone, an able Clerk of Works who later crops up repeatedly in connection with works in the garden. The church is often attributed today to the Bastard Brothers, the celebrated dynasty of builders of the nearby town of Blandford Forum, but they may have worked to the design of the Palladian architect Henry Flitcroft, a faithful protégé of both the 3rd Earl of Burlington and of William Kent. Flitcroft is certainly recorded as working at St Giles House by 1740, and an old family tradition asserts that he worked on both church and house.

On 19 March 1743, £100 was paid 'to Mr Flitcroft for surveying and making plans for St Giles House'. The plans appear to have included the design of the new lodges, which were erected in the summer the following year. The craftsmen named in the accounts give a good idea of the dramatis personae who were recruited to work on the house and garden in those years. The surprising number of London craftsmen shows the high quality and sophistication of the refurbishments. Thus, although 'Cartwright', the 'carver', mentioned in the building accounts for 1743, can be identified as the competent Blandford mason and builder Francis Cartwright, 'Phillips', the 'joiner', was probably John Phillips, who worked for Flitcroft fitting up houses in Berkeley Square in London. 'Bosson', the 'carver', is John Boson, a carver in wood and stone, who is recorded as working for William Kent near London at Kew, while 'Duval', the 'mason', can be identified as John Devall, a well-known London mason. In June 1744, the London sculptor Peter Scheemakers was paid £4 4s. 0d. for 'plaster heads'—probably the ornaments in the Great Dining Room cornice, while Aaron Jones painted and gilded the room later that year. The 'Mr Hallett' who received the enormous sum of £167 for carved chairs in May 1745 was the famous London cabinetmaker and upholsterer William Hallett.

Flitcroft's final recorded payment was in May 1746, but given the amount of work done at St Giles House, it is likely that much of the later documentation has been lost. In fact,

Flitcroft completely regularised St Giles House externally, skilfully uniting the red brick ranges built by Sir Anthony Ashley and the 1st Earl of Shaftesbury by raising them to a uniform height and articulating them with stone dressings in the classical taste. The evidence of Flitcroft's interventions, betrayed by the darker brickwork, can still be clearly seen on the fabric. Around the whole he ran a high parapet with bold crenellations, a curious antiquarian touch that may have been to emphasise the antiquity of the house and family. The transformation required drastic changes in level—on the north side of the house, Flitcroft created a broad terrace, raising the ground level so that the old Hall was relegated to the status of a basement room. A new main entrance was created on the raised ground floor, the site of the present-day Tapestry Room, marked externally by a projecting frontispiece, with a rusticated, pedimented doorway and a handsomely framed window above. Flitcroft also raised the ground level on the south side of house.

On the north, east and south fronts he regularised the windows to a uniform size and gave them stone surrounds, with aprons, keystones and voussoirs (wedge-shaped stones). Those windows on the upper level of the western half of the north front are in fact blind, so as to maintain symmetry while accommodating the vault of the Great Dining Room. The corners of all three fronts were articulated with cut stone quoins, while a grander stone doorcase, with a pediment enclosing an armorial cartouche, took the place of the 1st Earl's austere

opposite, left A short composition, or air, by the composer George Frideric Handel, written at St Giles around 1739.

opposite, right Portrait of George Frideric Handel, painted by Susannah, 4th Countess of Shaftesbury.

below, left Portrait by Joseph Highmore of Anthony, 4th Earl of Shaftesbury (1711–1771), in peer's robes.

below, right Portrait by Joseph Highmore of Susannah Noel (1710–1758), in peeress's robes. She was the only daughter of the 3rd Earl of Gainsborough and the first wife of the 4th Earl of Shaftesbury.

stone doorcase in the middle of the east front.

Inside the house, the most important interior was the fitting up of the Great Dining Room in that fusion of Palladian classicism with Rococo elements that Henry Flitcroft had made his own in suites of grand white and gold rooms at Wentworth Woodhouse, Yorkshire (1734), Ditchley Park, Oxfordshire (1736–41), Wimpole Hall in Cambridgeshire (1742–55) and Woburn Abbey, Bedfordshire (1747–61). Flitcroft's Great Room—it was a splendid, multipurpose saloon rather than a dedicated dining room—was richly decorated, dominated by a grandiose marble chimney piece with a columned, pedimented overmantel enclosing *The Bertie Boys*, a painting once attributed to Van Dyck but now thought to be by John Hayls. Around the walls, more family portraits set

in architectural frames alternated with pedimented door-cases and gilt-framed wall panels. Between the windows stood specially commissioned gilt-wood console tables and mirrors in the Rococo taste. Above, the high, coved ceiling was divided into three compartments enriched with gilded plasterwork. Next door, in the older part of the house, a Music Room, later called the White Hall, was created, with white-painted oak panelling of an architectural character, with blind arches and festoons of fruit and flowers. The plaster ceiling, again divided into compartments in the Palladian manner, is inhabited by Rococo flourishes. Flitcroft also remodelled the interior of the new entrance hall (now the Tapestry Room) but no trace of his work survives today. The 7th Earl claimed that his father remembered the room as having had a columned screen with two stone pillars.

Flitcroft's transformation of St Giles House was proudly commemorated by three views in John Hutchins's *The History and Antiquities of the County of Dorset* (1774). The first is B. Pryce's *Elevation of the East Front of Winbourne St Giles*, engraved by W. Walker, of about 1760, and there are also two near identical perspective views of the house and gardens from the south-east by Thomas Vivares of around the same time, showing the same view with and without the addition of the 1st Earl's old-fashioned terraces in the garden. Pryce's view perhaps derives from one of Flitcroft's lost design drawings, and it may have been executed whilst the works were still in progress. The Vivares views also show the three-storey service wing extending off to the south-west of the house. This survived, much altered and rebuilt, until the 1970s when it was demolished as part of the truncation of the house by the 10th Earl. Indeed, the service areas at St Giles House appear to have been much admired—Hutchins noted in 1774 'the apartments below stairs are esteemed the best in England'. Much of this was doubtless a result of Flitcroft's campaign of modernisation—there was even a Justice Room and accompanying cell under the south-west range for the administration of local law and order.

While the house was being recast, from about 1732 to 1750, works were going on in the garden and park. Here

again, although it is not certain, Flitcroft appears to have been involved in the design of at least some of the garden buildings. Whether a garden designer of the calibre of Charles Bridgeman, who worked with Flitcroft on the gardens of nearby Amesbury Abbey in the 1730s, was ever consulted is not known, although in 1734 a payment was made to 'Mr Dodington's gardener' at nearby Eastbury 'for making a plan of ye New Garden'. One 'John Barrett', who was paid for work on the Cascade in 1748, was probably the John Barrett recorded as working on the fountains and irrigation at Kensington Palace in the early eighteenth century, where Bridgeman was certainly employed. However, although Bridgeman could have inspired the formal terraces seen in one of the Vivares views, a garden of a very different spirit was laid out around the lake created by damming the River Allen in 1732–33. Here, around its banks, as well as planting cedars of Lebanon—some of which still survive—a circuit of ornamental buildings in a variety of whimsical styles was planned, possibly inspired by the Elysian Fields at Stowe, Buckinghamshire, laid out by William Kent from 1731, or Stourhead, Wiltshire, where Flitcroft designed several garden buildings from 1741 to the mid-1750s.

According to visitor Robert Andrew's journal for September 1752, exploring the garden from the south-west corner of the house, one first glimpsed the 'Castle on the Island', fortified by 'guns', passed through the 'Castellated Arch and Towers', and arrived at the Cascade. The Castellated Arch, he claimed, was inspired by a large Salvator Rosa landscape in the house. Further to the south one encountered Arethusa's Temple and then a Chinese Bridge, following the course of the Serpentine River until you reached an octagonal Thatched House on a low mount. Here the paths diverged, one easier and the other longer and more arduous—a clear reference to the 3rd Earl's *The Choice of Hercules*—both ending at the 'Pavilion on the Mount' in the Wilderness. The Wilderness also contained Shakespeare's Seat or House, which contained the original model for Peter Scheemakers's statue of the Bard which had been erected in Westminster Abbey in 1741—another project of 'Countess Susan' in her capacity of

South East View of Wimbourn St. Giles, the Seat of Anthony Ashley Cooper Earl of Shaftesbury.

foundress of the 'Shakespeare Ladies Club'. Lurking in the Wilderness was also a 'Root House' and 'Rootery Garden', a 'Hermitage', a 'Flint Arch', a 'Hermit's Cave' and finally the spectacular Grotto, the last building on the circuit walk. M.F. Billington, writing of St Giles House in *Historic Houses of the United Kingdom* (1892), suggests that a stream was originally intended to run through the Grotto: 'in the original design there was to have been water always running through it, but this notion was abandoned on account of the destructive influences of continuous damp'. Other features known to have existed in the grounds of St Giles House in the eighteenth century include an 'Eye Trap' (on Rye Hill), a 'Tent', a 'Sham Gate' and a 'Duck House'.

The first mention of the 'Castle on the Lake' in the accounts is in November 1744, while over the summer of the following year the faithful George Osboldestone supervised work on the Pavilion, Castle, Sham Gates and the Duck House. The Grotto is first mentioned in 1746 (although it probably occupies the site of an earlier grotto feature), and it was decorated, supposedly at the cost of ten thousand pounds,

in the autumn of that year. The gardens at St Giles House are evocatively described by Richard Pococke in *The Travels Through England of Richard Pococke ...* (1889), who visited on 6 October 1754:

The gardens are very beautifully laid out, in a serpentine river, pieces of water, lawns &c., and very gracefully adorn'd with wood. One first comes to an island in which there is a castle, then near the water is a gateway, with a tower on each side, and passing between two waters there is a fine cascade from one to the other, a thatch'd house, a round pavilion on a mount, Shake Spear's house, in which is a small statue of him, and his works in a glass case; and in all the houses and seats are books in hanging glass cases. There is a pavilion between the waters, and both a Chinese and a stone bridge over them. I saw here a sea duck which lays in rabbit's burrows, from which they are called burrow ducks, and are something like the shell drake. There is a most beautiful grotto finished by Mr. Castles of Marybone; it consists of a winding walk and an anti-room. These are

mostly made of rock spar &c, adorn'd with moss. In the
inner room is a great profusion of the most beautiful shells,
petrifactions, and fine polished pebbles, and there is a chim-
ney to it which is shut up with doors covered with shells, in
such a manner that it does not appear. The park also is very
delightful, and there is a building in it.

Another description is supplied in John Hutchins's *The His-*
tory and Antiquities of the County of Dorset (1774):

The garden is pleasant and spacious; the River Allen runs
through it, and it is adorned with several pieces of water,
pleasure houses, statues etc. here is one of the finest grot-
toes in England, which consists of two parts: the innermost
and largest furnished with a vast variety of curious shells
disposed in the most beautiful manner: the outer compart-
ment, or ante grotto, with ores and minerals of all kinds, col-
lected from various parts of the world. It was begun in 1751.
The arrangement took up two years and with the expense of
collecting the shells ores etc cost £10,000.

Eighteenth-century visitor Robert Andrew was particularly impressed by the Grotto, where he was shown an
unusual curiosity; 'a live Toad lately taken out of a large Block
of stone, w.ch was working up for y.e Building. There was a
spider found in the same cavity, who being glad to be released
from so disagreeable a companion made it's escape, as soon as
it got at Liberty'.

The death of the Countess of Shaftesbury in 1758 seems
to have caused a pause in the improvements to the house
and gardens at St Giles House, although in 1759 the 4th Earl
married a second time, to Mary Bouverie, second daughter
of the 1st Viscount Folkestone, who bore two sons. In 1764, a
further bout of activity saw the addition to the garden circuit
of a pedimented Ionic aedicule, the Temple of Aresthusa
and Thomson's Seat (named after a friend of the 4th Earl
and his first Countess—the famous poet James Thomson,
author of *The Seasons*). Lord Shaftesbury also established
White, Green and Great Pheasantries—wooden latticework
structures, with little lanterns on their roofs, each intended
to house pheasants as described by its name. On his death in

1771, the 4th Earl was succeeded by the eldest son, Anthony, 5th Earl of Shaftesbury (1761–1811), who married Barbara, daughter of Sir John Webb, 5th Baronet of Odstock, Wiltshire. They consulted the architect Sir John Soane about further improvements to the house—Soane visited in November 1793, submitting plans the following year, but these do not survive. The architect Thomas Cundy took over, supervising, in 1810, the rendering of the external brickwork of the house and throwing together the rooms of the second state apartment— the Great Parlour, Drawing Room and Ante-room—to form a 65-foot-long Library. This renovation was to have included a primitive chair lift in a lobby at its eastern end, presumably to allow his patron, who suffered from ill health, access to the Library from the bedrooms above, although the 5th Earl's death in May 1811 made this unnecessary. Cundy was recalled between 1813 and 1820 to carry out more ambitious works for the 5th Earl's heir and younger brother, Cropley Ashley, the 6th Earl (1768–1851), and his grand wife, Anne, a daughter of the 4th Duke of Marlborough. This included completing the Library, which was subdivided by a pair of scagliola columns (in imitation of stone), and the covering over of the courtyard in the centre of the house to form the lofty Saloon or Stone Hall. This imposing space, its lantern supported by a starfish vault, is so similar to the one Soane proposed at Chillington Hall in Staffordshire in 1786 that it might possibly embody some of his ideas from a decade earlier. The construction of the Stone Hall necessitated the destruction of the Great Staircase, so Cundy inserted the present, somewhat vertiginous, staircase topped with a lantern in the narrow space that remained. Meanwhile, a gallery around three sides of the Stone Hall improved access to the upper floors on the western side of the house. Many of the rooms were redecorated at this time, the North and South Drawing Rooms were hung with striped silk, and many of the upstairs rooms were papered.

A curious story may explain the covering over of the courtyard and the destruction of the 1st Earl's Great Staircase. It is said that the creation of the Stone Hall at St Giles House was galvanised by the acquisition of a magnificent 'machine organ' by the 5th Earl of Shaftesbury. This impressive instrument, which had been commissioned from John Snetzler by the 3rd Earl of Bute for Luton Hoo in Bedfordshire some twenty-five years before, and perfected by a watchmaker called Alexander Cumming, had some sixty musical barrels, each over four feet long, which could play works by Handel, Corelli and other composers. After Lord Bute's death in 1792, his heirs attempted to install the organ in other houses belonging to the family, but the instrument was eventually acquired by Lord Shaftesbury. When it was installed at St Giles House it was found that there was no place to store the barrels, so the staircase had to be removed to make room for them, and a new, narrower stair was erected in an adjoining lightwell. The new staircase suffered from structural problems and had to be dismantled, and when the 5th Earl returned from a sojourn abroad he found that he had no access at all to the upper floors of his house. On his death, his heirs sold the monstrous instrument back to its creator, Cumming, at a knock-down price. This may explain why Thomas Cundy returned to make further alterations in this part of the house for the 6th Earl.

The next major alterations to St Giles House were carried out by the 7th Earl, who succeeded to the title and estates in 1853. Anthony Ashley-Cooper was born in 1801, the eldest son of the 6th Earl, although by all accounts his relationship with his parents was distant and loveless, and he was traumatised by his brutal experiences at school. His miserable childhood was ameliorated by a kindly housekeeper, whose simple Christianity provided for the boy a model of Christian love that would form the basis for much of his later social activism and philanthropic work. A serious and conscientious young man, he entered Parliament in 1826, while still studying at Oxford. His earliest campaigns included the reform of the lunacy laws, which he investigated with great energy on Parliamentary Select Committees, uncovering many scandalous abuses. This culminated in the two great Lunacy Acts of 1845, and it was a cause to which he was devoted throughout his life. Another preoccupation was to end the exploitation of child labour, with his Ten Hour Act, first introduced to Parliament in 1833 but only passed in 1847, followed by a campaign

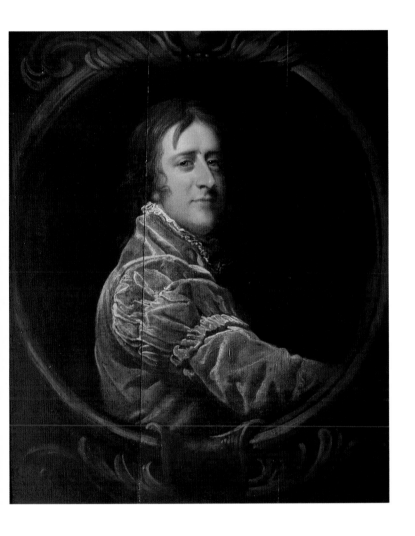

opposite Portrait by Pompeo Girolamo Batoni of Anthony, 5th Earl of Shaftesbury (1761–1811), leaning on a plinth with the Ludovisi Ares.

above, left Portrait by Richard Cosway of Cropley, 6th Earl of Shaftesbury (1768–1851).

above, right Portrait by Richard Cosway of Anne Spencer (1773–1865), fourth daughter of the 4th Duke of Marlborough and wife of Cropley, 6th Earl of Shaftesbury.

to outlaw the exploitative employment of women and children in the mines. Campaigns against other abuses followed, including improving the lot of chimney sweeps, the Ragged School Union movement and the suppression of the Chinese opium trade, as well as his crusade for the establishment of a permanent home for the Jews in the Holy Land. Lord Shaftesbury is remembered even today as one of the greatest philanthropists of Victorian Britain. On his death in 1885, the Earl was buried not in Westminster Abbey, where his funeral service took place attended by vast crowds, but at his own wish in the family vault in the Parish Church at Wimborne St Giles. Apart from his formidable legacy of social reforms, the 7th Earl is commemorated by the famous Shaftesbury Memorial in Piccadilly Circus in London. Designed by Sir Alfred Gilbert and erected in 1893, it takes the form of a fountain surmounted by a statue of a winged genius—not Eros, as he is popularly known, but Anteros, symbol of selfless love. A recent cast of this figure, made from a mould taken from the original, has been acquired by the present Lord Shaftesbury to decorate the new formal garden facing the east front at St Giles House.

Lord Shaftesbury's architectural patronage was perhaps less successful than his philanthropic career. Shaftesbury, then styled Lord Ashley, had married in 1830 Lady Emily Cowper, daughter of the 5th Earl Cowper, who brought her husband advantageous political connexions through her maternal uncle, Lord Melbourne, and her stepfather (and possibly biological father) Lord Palmerston. They produced a large family of ten children, and perhaps it was this expansion that encouraged Shaftesbury, after he inherited the title and estates in 1853, to employ the young Philip Charles Hardwick to remodel St Giles House. It is said that the works were paid for by Lord Shaftesbury's sister, Lady Caroline Neeld, a rich and childless widow. Shaftesbury was convinced that he was perpetually on the brink of financial ruin, and his own resources were almost entirely devoted to making improvements to the living conditions of his estate workers. His architect, P.C. Hardwick, was the scion of a great dynasty of architects, the son of Philip Hardwick and grandson of Thomas Hardwick. He proposed

above, top Daughters of the 7th Earl and Countess of Shaftesbury outside the South Drawing Room bay window: Lady Edith Ashley-Cooper, Lady Victoria Ashley-Cooper and Lady Constance Ashley-Cooper.

above, bottom The same group as above with the 7th Earl and Countess of Shaftesbury, Lady Harriet Ashley-Cooper and granddaughter Margaret.

below, left Marble bust by Matthew Noble of the 7th Earl of Shaftesbury, presented to his wife, Emily, by the Labourers of the Manufacturing Districts of the North of England in 1859.

below, right Inscription on the plinth of the 7th Earl's bust—a tribute to his dedication to factory reform during the nineteenth century, in particular the Ten Hours Act.

opposite The Shaftesbury Memorial, by sculptor Sir Alfred Gilbert and unveiled in London in 1893, is known as 'Eros' and represents the selfless love of the 7th Earl of Shaftesbury. It was the first statue in the world to be cast from aluminium, and is set on a bronze base. This figure was cast in the 1980s from the original mould as part of an edition of ten. The sculpture in the Sunk Garden at St Giles House faces in the direction of its counterpart in Piccadilly Circus, London.

a comprehensive rebuilding of the western half of the house, with two large towers to the north and south, topped by steeply pitched mansard roofs in the French manner. Beneath the North Tower, an arcaded portico of rusticated stonework crowned with ball finials became the main entrance to the house. Hardwick's aim was to give a picturesque silhouette to what must have been considered then a rather unfashionable, squatly proportioned, classical mansion. Hardwick had just built the Great Western Hotel at Paddington Station in London, completed in 1852 but much altered since, which had

a pair of somewhat similar mansard-roofed towers. Towers in fact became something of a Hardwick country house trademark, ranging from the solitary, mansard-crowned, vertical features at the Abbotts at Sompting in Sussex (1856) or Adare Manor, Co. Limerick (complete by 1862), to the hectic skyline of Addington Manor, Buckinghamshire (1857). But these were either new country houses or additions to recent ones. At St Giles House, Hardwick's decision to graft an evocation of part of the Tuileries Palace on to the largely Carolean house seems both ungainly and unwise. However, it is hard to

PRESENTED TO

EMILY

WIFE OF THE SEVENTH

EARL OF SHAFTESBURY

BY THE OPERATIVES

OF THE MANUFACTORING DISTRICTS

OF THE NORTH OF ENGLAND

AS A TOKEN OF ESTEEM AND REGARD

FOR THE PERSEVERING

AND SUCCESSFUL EFFORTS

OF HER NOBLE HUSBAND

IN PROMOTING

BY LEGISLATIVE ENACTMENT

A LIMITATION OF THE HOURS OF LABOUR

OF CHILDREN FEMALES

AND YOUNG PERSONS

EMPLOYED IN MILLS AND FACTORIES.

AUGUST 6TH 1859.

St Giles House in 1868. The building shows the new attic floor with
dormer windows, the mansard-roofed towers and the bay windows
added by architect P.C. Hardwick. In the foreground, the future
8th Earl of Shaftesbury, here as Lord Ashley, stands in leather
boots and a hat, with other family members and friends.

1868

opposite A page from the 8th Earl of Shaftesbury's family photo album, showing him as Lord Ashley in the centre, surrounded by his parents, the 7th Earl and Countess of Shaftesbury; his eldest daughter Margaret; his nurse Miss Toomer; Lady Constance Ashley-Cooper; Lady Templemore (previously Lady Victoria Ashley-Cooper); Viscountess Palmerston (the mother of Emily, Countess of Shaftesbury) and his wife, Lady Harriet Chichester (later the 8th Countess of Shaftesbury).

below St Giles Church and almshouses in the village of Wimborne St Giles. The church was modified in 1887 by George Frederick Bodley and then again in 1908 by the architect Ninian Comper after a fire damaged much of the interior. The almshouses were built by Sir Anthony Ashley in 1624.

appreciate today how much many mid-Victorian landowners detested the 'insipid' architectural taste of their forebears.

Hardwick was also active within St Giles House, converting the former entrance hall into a Tapestry Room, installing here the three seventeenth-century Brussels tapestries, made in the workshop of Albert Auwercx, depicting the Triumphs of the Gods, and sweeping away most of Flitcroft's decoration, including a screen of stone columns. There were also alterations to the Library, which involved removing the 6th Earl's scagliola columns to make way for new bookcases, and the addition of a large, projecting window bay in 1853–54. A second bay window was added to the South Drawing Room, and there were alterations to the bedrooms upstairs. The 7th Earl

also carried out work in the gardens, creating a broad terrace, studded with vases and topiary, around the house, and laying out a formal parterre, centred on a fountain, beneath the East front. He also added a 'pinetum' to the pleasure grounds. The parish Church of Wimborne St Giles was also partly gothicised by the ecclesiastical architect George Frederick Bodley in 1887, receiving two aisles and a nave chapel.

Hardwick's additions to St Giles House soon began giving trouble. According to the 7th Earl:

> *The north wing was pulled down (being in a ruinous state) and rebuilt ... Mr Holland was the builder and Mr Hardwick the architect. And ditto of the alteration of the library and*

the rooms above. It was shamefully done as may be seen by the settlements in the portico, on the court side of the north wing and the state of the long room doors. There are also two slight fissures in the ceiling of the library. I have left all of these as proof of the neglect of Mr Hardwick the architect, omitted altogether to supervise the builder. I refused in consequence to pay him more than £200.

These structural problems, which may have been caused by the culverted stream that ran beneath the western end of the house, proved insoluble. Hardwick's troublesome mansard roofs were finally taken down in 1886, just after the death of the 7th Earl, during the tenure of his eldest son, Anthony (1831–1886), a naval captain who briefly presided at St Giles House as the 8th Earl, committing suicide six months after succeeding to the title. Shorn of their high roofs, the stumps of the towers were neatly finished off by balustrading and stone ball finials.

Before he inherited as the 8th Earl, Captain Ashley-Cooper had married, in 1857, Lady Harriet Chichester, only daughter and heiress of the 3rd Marquess of Donegall. She brought extensive estates in the north of Ireland to the family, and paid for further improvements to the park and gardens,

although her father-in-law blamed her for his son's extravagance and called her 'hard-hearted, insolent, mean, tyrannical and ungrateful'. She died in Rome in 1898. The 8th Earl was succeeded by his son, Anthony, the 9th Earl (1869–1961), whose long and eventful tenure spanned seven monarchs, two world wars and tumultuous social change. The new Earl had to contend from the start with extensive remedial work to the house. In 1890, it had to be almost entirely re-roofed by a firm of builders called Franklin, at the cost of £2,000. A completely new drainage system was devised by Dr Corfield, while Messrs Easton and Anderson of Whitehall Place, London installed a new water supply. In 1892 St Giles House was let to E.B. Portman for three years—Lord Shaftesbury's duties as lieutenant in the 10th Hussars, and, from 1895, aide-de-camp to the Governor of the Australian state of Victoria, meant he was frequently absent. The house was let completely furnished; all the bedrooms were extensively refurnished by Messrs Hampton of Pall Mall, while the agents' particulars breathlessly describe the 'numerous works of art, statuary etc and a quantity of genuine Chippendale furniture'.

Lord Shaftesbury's retirement from the regular army and marriage to Lady Constance Grosvenor in 1899 was accompanied by an influx of money. Electric light was installed at

opposite, left Portrait of Anthony, 9th Earl of Shaftesbury (1869–1961), in the uniform of the 10th Royal Hussars. Painted in 1894 by Hermann Schmiechen.

opposite, right Portrait by Sir James Jebusa Shannon of Lady Constance Sibell Grosvenor (1875–1957), daughter of Earl Grosvenor and wife of the 9th Earl of Shaftesbury.

below Plaque from the Army Council 'in the name of the Nation', thanking the family for use of St Giles House as a military infirmary during the First World War.

bottom School photograph of the pupils and teachers of Miss Faunce's Academy, which took up residence at the house during the Second World War, with the 9th Earl and Countess of Shaftesbury.

St Giles House in 1900, while it was around this time that the *décor chinois*, French panoramic wallpaper to a design first made by Zuber in 1832, was hung in the Japan Room, where it still in part survives. The Prince and Princess of Wales (the future King George V and Queen Mary) stayed at St Giles House in 1907—Lord Shaftesbury served as Chamberlain to the Queen both before and after her husband's accession to the throne—and there were endless house parties, shoots and hunt balls. In 1908, after a disastrous fire, the distinguished ecclesiastical architect Sir Ninian Comper restored the parish church with great sensitivity, and went on to conjure up a pretty little Gothic Revival chapel out of the old Justice Room in the centre of the south-west service wing for the Earl's High Church wife. During the First World War Lord Shaftesbury enlisted again, this time as commander of the 1st South Western Mounted Brigade, and served throughout, retiring with the rank of Honorary Brigadier General in 1919. Meanwhile, parts of the house were used as a hospital.

In 1943, St Giles House was featured in an article in *Country Life*. The photographs show the house in good condition and fully furnished, seemingly in its heyday. In fact, by the time it was published the Second World War was raging and Lord and Lady Shaftesbury had retreated to a wing of the emptied house. Most of it was occupied by a school, Miss Faunce's Academy, a progressive Parent National Education School which had been evacuated from London. In fact, it could have been worse; the approximately seventy-five blue-blooded little girls were generally well behaved, kept in order by a host of teachers and matrons who were in fact their governesses and nannies. Lord Shaftesbury once again enlisted into the army, this time as a private in the Home Guard—Captain Carter, the head gamekeeper, was his commanding officer. After the war, Lord Shaftesbury attempted to keep the house going, but 'domestic servants are practically unobtainable', he wrote. 'Girls nowadays will not have anything to say to domestic service and footmen no longer exist—with the result that these large houses are no longer practical propositions to live in. What is to become of the old family house where successive generations have lived for so

Françoise Soulier, wife of Anthony Ashley-Cooper, Lord Ashley, with their two children, Anthony, later 10th Earl of Shaftesbury, and Lady Frances Ashley-Cooper.

long is impossible to foretell.' The couple moved to the dower house, but after Lady Shaftesbury's death in 1957, Lord Shaftesbury—then in his eighties—moved back into the big house, opening it occasionally to the public in the summer. He died, aged 91, in 1961.

The 9th Earl and his wife had two sons and four daughters, but the Earl outlived his eldest son and heir, Anthony, Lord Ashley, who died prematurely from heart disease in 1947. Lord Ashley, who worked in the Intelligence Corps during the war, had married twice, firstly—to the horror of his family—to Sylvia Hawkes, an adventuress and showgirl, whom he divorced in 1934, with the American actor Douglas Fairbanks Sr. being named as co-respondent in the divorce petition. Lady Ashley went on to marry Fairbanks, and then a succession of three more husbands: the 6th Lord Sheffield, Clark Gable and Prince Dimitri Jorjadze. Lord Ashley's second wife, French-born Françoise Soulier, whom he married in 1937, bore two children, including a son, Anthony, who eventually inherited the title and the greatly reduced Shaftesbury estates—acres of land in Ireland and Dorset had to be sold to pay death duties.

Anthony Ashley-Cooper, 10th Earl of Shaftesbury (1938–2004), inherited St Giles House from his grandfather in 1961 when he was twenty-two years old. His own father had died when he was only eight, and his French mother, Françoise, had returned to live in Paris and married Col. François Goussault in 1947. Lord Shaftesbury and his sister, Lady Frances Ashley-Cooper, grew up travelling between France and St Giles House. He attended Eton and afterwards, briefly, studied in Oxford, but left to join the Royal Armoured Corps in 1957. He later transferred to the 10th Royal Hussars, before leaving the army to manage his estates. Once established in Dorset he became a respected conservationist, planting a million trees, presiding over conservation charities such as the Hawk and Owl Trust and the British Butterfly Conservation Trust, and he was joint winner of the Royal Forestry Society's award for Forestry and Conservation. He also served as the Chairman of the London Philharmonic Orchestra between 1966 and 1980, and was President of the Shaftesbury Society, the charity founded by his great-great-grandfather, the 7th Earl of Shaftesbury.

Lord Shaftesbury married his first wife, Bianca, in 1966, and threw himself into the work of reviving St Giles House, which by this time was in a poor state of repair. His plans to restore the house involved cutting it down to a more manageable size—returning it to its eighteenth-century form—and adapting it for modern living. Advice was taken, and in 1971 work began on the demolition of the north wing and part of the south wing, including the stump of the truncated Hardwick tower over the north front and its arcaded portico. Decaying nineteenth-century cement render was also chipped away from the brickwork of the main house, and the 7th Earl's incongruous bay windows were removed. Within the house, drastic measures were taken to cut away areas affected by dry and wet rot, including the removal of half the Palladian plasterwork in Flitcroft's Great Dining Room, while the house attics were extensively stripped out and reorganised in an attempt to return them to their pre-Hardwick state. The work continued for several years, and then came to an abrupt halt, as the funds ran out due to the difficult economic climate in the mid-1970s and a failed property deal, leaving parts of the house virtually open to the

below Anthony, 10th Earl of Shaftesbury, leading a horse around the south side of St Giles House, about 1970.

overleaf Aerial view of St Giles House and Park, about 1950.

elements. Lord Shaftesbury's divorce from his first wife in 1976, and his remarriage to Christina Montan, the daughter of a Swedish diplomat, may have taken his attention away from the restoration project, as would the birth of their two sons, Anthony and Nicholas, in 1977 and 1979 respectively. Faced with seemingly unsurmountable problems with the house, he gradually lost interest in the project and its momentum was lost. Thinking it unlikely that the house would ever be reoccupied, some of the best pictures, furniture and other heirlooms were consigned to Christie's auction rooms in June 1980. The departure of the carved and gilded mirrors and console tables which had been designed for the house, most of the celebrated St Giles House suite of seat furniture,

and key family pictures such as Paolo de' Matteis's *The Choice of Hercules*, commissioned in 1711 in Naples by the 3rd Earl of Shaftesbury, with its extraordinary Rococo frame, were grievous losses to the Shaftesbury inheritance. Luckily, Lord Shaftesbury was talked out of sending all the remaining family portraits to the saleroom. After this, St Giles House sank into a deep sleep, and the shuttered, half-ruined building, surrounded by its overgrown gardens with its silted-up lake and decaying ornamental garden buildings, made a memorable impression. However, gradually this state of romantic *dishabille* gave way to squalid decay. The Grotto, which had been painstakingly restored by Mrs Jebb and Miss Sant as recently as 1959, became boarded up and dangerous,

its curiously designed furniture stolen, its shells and spars pilfered by trespassers.

A further blow came in 1999, when Lord Shaftesbury divorced his second wife and moved out of Mainsail Haul, leaving her and their eldest son to manage the estate. Lord Shaftesbury moved to France, living a peripatetic life between Versailles and the Côte d'Azur, much to the concern of his family and friends. He was reported missing in November 2004, and subsequent police investigations and trial led to the conviction, in 2007, of Jamila M'Barak, whom he had married in 2002, and her brother for his murder. Lord Shaftesbury's body was recovered and interred in the family crypt at Wimborne St Giles in September 2005, next to his eldest son, Anthony, who had briefly inherited as the 11th Earl of Shaftesbury, but had died suddenly from a heart attack in New York in May 2005, aged 27, only six months after assuming the title.

His younger brother, Nicholas Ashley-Cooper, thus unexpectedly inherited as the 12th Earl of Shaftesbury. Born in 1979, he had been working as a successful DJ and music promoter in New York, but returned to England in 2005 to assume his responsibilities after the two terrible family tragedies—or as he puts it, 'to step up to the plate'. One of these was to decide what to do about St Giles House, which had been deteriorating for years and was on English Heritage's (now Historic England) Buildings at Risk register since 2001. As far back as 2003, the family Trustees had commissioned specialist conservation surveyor Philip Hughes to prepare a detailed condition report and undertake emergency repairs to the fabric in an enlightened collaboration with English Heritage. As part of this project, Susie Barson and John Cattell of English Heritage prepared a comprehensive report on the building, making use of new historical research and the physical evidence uncovered during a detailed structural survey of the partially stripped interior. This informed the work of restoring the house, and was indeed a great help in the writing of this chapter. Meanwhile, the new Lord Shaftesbury had been studying for an MBA at the London Business School, so as to help prepare him for running the family estates. He

married, in 2010, Dinah Streifeneder, a veterinary surgeon, and just over a year later they moved back into St Giles House, to a self-contained apartment in the south wing, so as to be on hand during what would be a four-year restoration of the entire building. This was carried out under the direction of Philip Hughes by Ellis & Co., a leading traditional West Country building contractor. Now complete, the restoration of St Giles House has deservedly won several national awards for the conservation of historic buildings, including the 2015 Georgian Group Award for the restoration of a country house, the 2015 Royal Institute of Chartered Surveyors Award for Building Conservation and the 2015 Historic Houses Association/Sotheby's Restoration Award. The work was carried out in three phases, the last being the building of a new block on the site of the demolished Victorian North Tower, with the new front door proudly proclaimed by an impressive rusticated Doric loggia. The park and gardens of St Giles House have also been extensively restored, guided by the researches of Suzannah Fleming. Work has included dredging the lake, replanting the avenue and reinstating the formal garden, to a new design, below the east front. The surviving garden buildings have also been restored, including the Grotto, once on the verge of collapse, which has been made safe, and its mollusc and spar embellishments reinstated by Sally Strachey in 2014. Thus restored, St Giles House is now very much home to Lord and Lady Shaftesbury and their three children, while the former state rooms have been sensitively refurbished with the advice of Edward Hurst, retaining wherever possible the distressed old paintwork and wallpapers. Now splendidly but sparsely furnished with the surviving family portraits and furniture, some of them given back by friends and family members, they are used to host a wide variety of events, ranging from weddings to literary festivals, which help the house to earn its keep. But the story of the triumphant revival of St Giles House has already been told by Lord Shaftesbury in his own words in the first part of this book.

EPILOGUE

It felt felt like the project was coming to a conclusion in 2015 when the North Tower work was complete and the Ellis and Co. site cabins were leaving the premises. This also coincided with the birth of our second daughter, Zara. In 2014 and 2015 the project won several conservation awards, which was a huge honour for us. Whilst this was not the reason we set out to do the work, it felt like deserved recognition for all the people who had been involved in restoring St Giles House and the hard work they had put in. We were lucky that the team remained relatively consistent throughout the years, and I believe that this consistency produced formidable results. St Giles House today is a testament to their work, skill and endeavour, which is all on display in this book.

Looking back, it still feels inconceivable that we managed to get as far as we have. I look at old photographs and think we must have been slightly mad to take the project on; but we are grateful that we did, because now St Giles is a living, breathing house again. When we started, our ambitions were modest, and we thought progress would be slow. However, as soon as we started, the momentum carried us forward and we became focused on getting the house to a point where it could start generating an income. We created an incredible bond with the house which has continued to this day and will carry us into the future.

Wherever we look there is more work to be done. By the time this book is published more projects will have been started and some finished. Further work completed in the house includes the creation of a bar and nightclub in the beer cellar for our events. We have also converted the seventeenth-century Riding House into eight-bedroom accommodation to support the events in the house. The experience we have gained from working on St Giles has helped us approach these projects with much more confidence.

It brings us a lot of pleasure that we are now able to share St Giles with the wider world through weddings, concerts, festivals, talks and tours. Without these events a lot of the house would not be seen or appreciated. Crucially, it also brings us the income we need to keep the place going.

However, alongside our commercial endeavours, we try to ensure that the house doesn't lose its role as a family home, which is our greatest priority. In this way, we hope our children will establish a love for the place, which will make them want to keep it going for the next generation. I feel lucky that we are living in a period where there are more opportunities for large country houses than when my father inherited, but I don't doubt there will be plenty more challenges ahead. Looking back over its history, many members of my family have had their struggles keeping the place going, but somehow they have found a way, and in doing so they have put so much of their energy and love into the house, which is what makes it such a special place today.

NICK ASHLEY-COOPER
12th Earl of Shaftesbury, October 2017

A portrait by Sir Joshua Reynolds of Mary Bouverie (1730–1804), third daughter of the 1st Viscount Folkestone and second wife of the 4th Earl of Shaftesbury, appears from behind a cardboard wrapper.

PHOTOGRAPHING
ST GILES HOUSE

Sadly, other than the thrill of realising that this would be a career-changing commission, there are only three things I can remember about the phone call that I received back in 2008. Firstly, that the family were keen for me to photograph at St Giles House whilst Lord and Lady Shaftesbury were away—with the prints being a Christmas present for Lord Shaftesbury. Secondly, that I was in the middle of stripping the wallpaper in my own tiny home when the call arrived. The memory of the mental effort needed for a little DIY was an excellent yardstick of how much energy it must have taken to carry a project on a huge, but unknown, scale. Thirdly, that one of the last things I was told was 'be very careful where you put your feet!' This advice certainly proved useful.

I had just three weeks to complete the work and I quickly realised that I would need almost all this time for a clear vision for the photography to coalesce. The house presented several problems for a photographer. The first was access. There had been some emergency propping done in the 1970s and 1980s that gave the impression that the structure was not altogether safe. Much of the exquisite plasterwork was hanging precariously, and the last thing I wanted to do was to break or damage anything. Many floorboards were up (or loose) and one of the wings of the house had been taken down, leaving some hastily erected boarding and a couple of precipitous drops.

None of this would have been a problem if it had been possible to walk around with the light coming through the windows, but the rooms were filled with huge quantities of furniture, boxes and a vast array of other objects that sometimes covered the closed shutters leaving no possibility of a simple series of open views of the rooms. There was a wholly inadequate series of lights, strung in the first few rooms to allow the narrow passages between the biggest items of furniture to be navigated.

But where there are restrictions in photography there are often opportunities. The house had not been properly explored for many decades and what remained was sparkling gold dust for the imagination. Who left the house and when? The furniture and paintings were obviously great treasures that had been unseen for at least a generation and the dilapidation of the rooms around them provided a mournful backdrop, but often one of elegant decay. By following the shafts of light that came through the cracks in the shutters and boards, focusing on small vignettes and using very long exposures, a photographic style that suited the subject became apparent over this first visit. I felt privileged to be able to tell the fullest photographic story of the house since it had last been occupied nearly fifty years earlier.

The rooms had been unused for decades, and not only was the dust thicker than any I had ever seen (which caused plenty of problems with my large-format film camera), but the stacks of objects made it difficult to guess what lay underneath. The experience of creeping through the vast house in the gloom, picking one's way amid the piles of priceless artefacts whilst avoiding the many unsafe paths felt akin, I imagined, to being an explorer or archeologist. The details that presented themselves contrasted beautifully with the backdrop of the fabric of the house itself. Old pictures, letters, toys and notes from decades before provided a powerful human connection, but it was often in the odd juxtaposition of the objects that one felt the sense of a house suspended in time. With artworks on the floor, some of them partially boxed, and large paintings and prints leaning against the walls, there was no doubt that one was truly working behind the scenes.

The damp had ravaged the building, but even then the self-stripping wallpaper gave a sense of times lost, and the flaking paint appeared like a kind of patina to the plaster. I believe the British have a strong sense of nostalgia for these houses, which are a significant part of our story. Many historic decisions were made within their walls, but also many lives lived, not just those of the aristocratic family at their core, but also those of the staff below stairs.

When the photographs were shown to Lord and Lady Shaftesbury they were enormously positive and encouraging. They almost immediately asked me to photograph the first restoration works, which would make a wing habitable for them and their family.

When talking with many of the artisans who worked on the restoration, I was often told it would be 'a life's work'. Indeed, the enormity of such a project appeared at the time to be feasible only for a national body; a pair of individuals taking on something like this seemed almost far-fetched. We would all be proven wrong.

The style of the in-progress photography followed that of the original series. I embraced the apparent mess and chaos and aimed to show the beauty of the craftsmanship. Whether that was the complex wiring and plumbing, plasterwork or painting, each has its own skill and style to be laid bare. I believe the dust, dirt and grime is intrinsic to the work and therefore intrinsic to understanding how the work is achieved.

Where more of the room was visible, I opened the view a little wider to show how work had progressed since the first series, but always with a view to showing how beautiful a building site can be, especially when everything is bespoke and a highly skilled, sympathetic renovation is underway. Even more wonderful was that through the removal of the top layer of the fabric of the house, whether that be the floorboards, plaster or wallpaper, it became possible to see the traces of the work of previous generations of artisans.

The atmosphere of the photographs was intended to be calm, contemplative and perhaps even a little detached to give a sense of place and time. While the heroes of the work might be the craftspeople, the portrait I needed to capture was that of the house itself. I hope the personalities of those who worked there can be seen in the tools and the traces of the works being done, but the star of the show was always the building. Nonetheless, in the recent photographs of the finished rooms I have brought in warmth and colour, now that the house has fully returned to its rightful state as a vibrant, living family home.

JUSTIN BARTON

EVOLUTION OF ST GILES HOUSE

The story of St Giles House is one of continual change over the centuries, with almost every generation adding and adapting something. This series of drawings shows the major architectural shifts from the early sixteenth century through to the present day. Thanks are due to John Cattell and Andy Crispe from Historic England for producing the drawings and for the accompanying information.

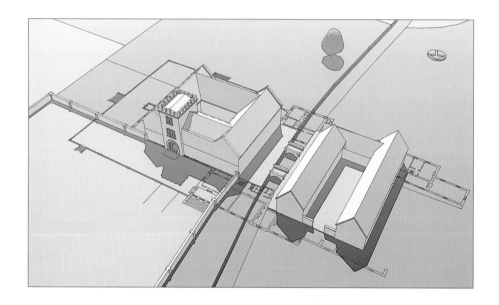

Early to mid-sixteenth century

A conjectural representation of the first manor house on the site. The U-plan service buildings to the west of the stream may be later in date but are depicted in this form in William Palmer's 1659 plan of the house and park. The house was approached from the north via an outer court which in the sixteenth century may have been enclosed by buildings.

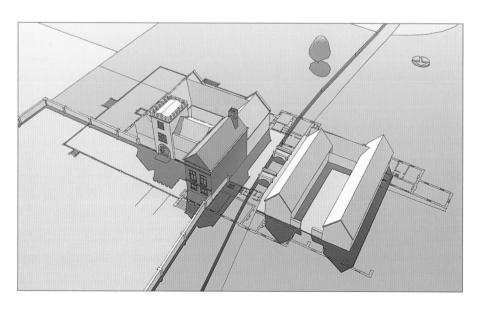

About 1639–43

The first of the new blocks is constructed on the site of the partially demolished old house and is where the White Hall and entrance vestibule are now located.

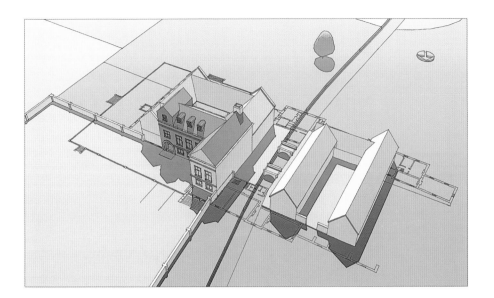

About 1645

The old north range is replaced by a new block containing the Great Dining Room and an entrance tower, possibly a reworking of an earlier gatehouse, with a carriage archway through to the inner court. The archway has a mid-sixteenth-century doorway inside the opening on its east side.

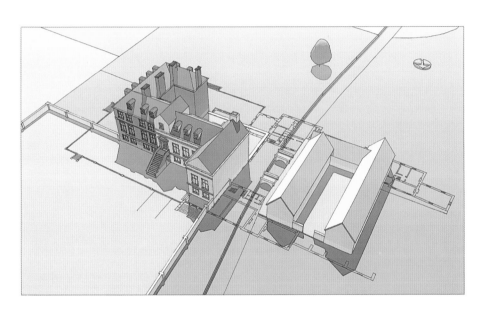

1650–59

A third block, the taller U-plan east section, is added. It incorporates a suite of high-status rooms on the principal floor. The main entrance was at principal floor level accessed from the court by a flight of stairs.

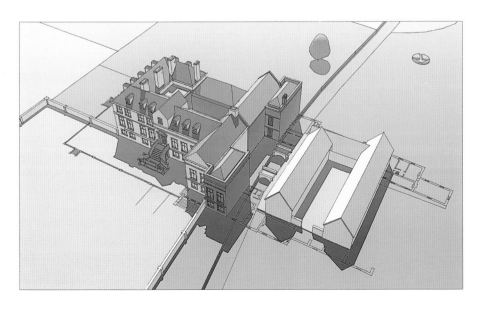

1670–72

A new block, lower in height, is added to the south, and a taller range to the south-west corner, possibly incorporating the part of the earlier house that became the servants' hall and Green Room. Also at this time there was a partial infilling of the inner court to create a Great Staircase compartment in the area between the rear wings of the 1650s east block. Narrow projecting blocks adjoining the stream were added between 1659 and 1672. A 'Great stone stair' led from the court to the entrance on the principal floor by that date.

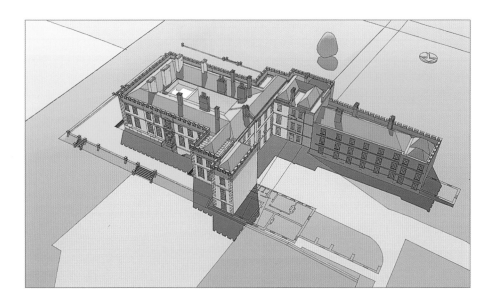

About 1735–50

The old service buildings to the west of the stream were demolished, a new west service range added in their place, and the water course culverted under the house and to the new lake. A new terrace around the north, east and south sides of the house relegated the old ground floor to a full basement, and a new north door, crenellated parapet and new roof were added, all to the designs of Henry Flitcroft.

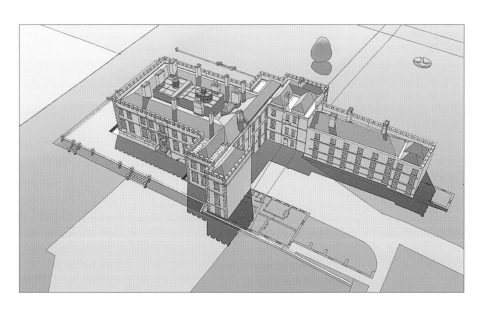

About 1813

The inner court was roofed over by Thomas Cundy to form the Stone Hall lit by a large oval lantern.

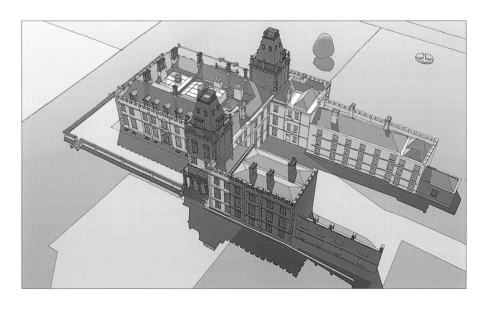

1854

The north-west service range is added, replacing an earlier (possibly early nineteenth-century) range in the same position, along with a wall to screen the partially open service court. There are two new towers with mansard roofs, and an entrance porch was created at the foot of the north tower. The house was re-roofed at that time and given a steeper pitch. All of this work was by P.C. Hardwick.

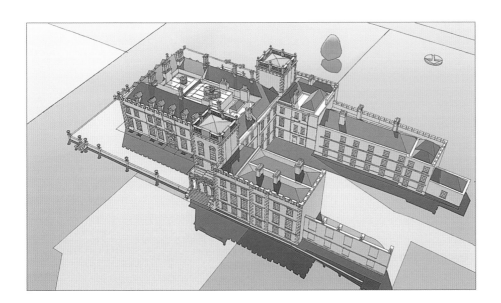

About 1886 to the early twentieth century

The mansard roofs over both the north and south towers were removed.

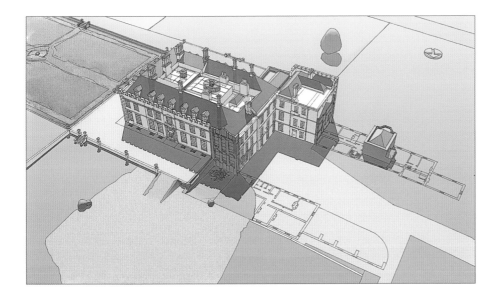

About 1973

The north and south service ranges were demolished and the North Tower and entrance removed. The South Tower was reduced in height.
The chapel was saved and a roof added to it, resulting in a detached building to the west of the house.

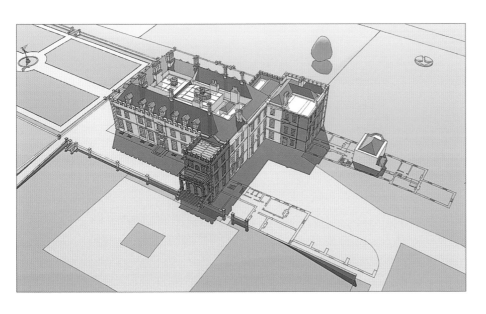

2018

Restoration of the house has included a new northern entrance block with a porch and steps. This addition helped restore the balance of the elevations and hide the exposed internal wall created by the demolition of the North Tower.

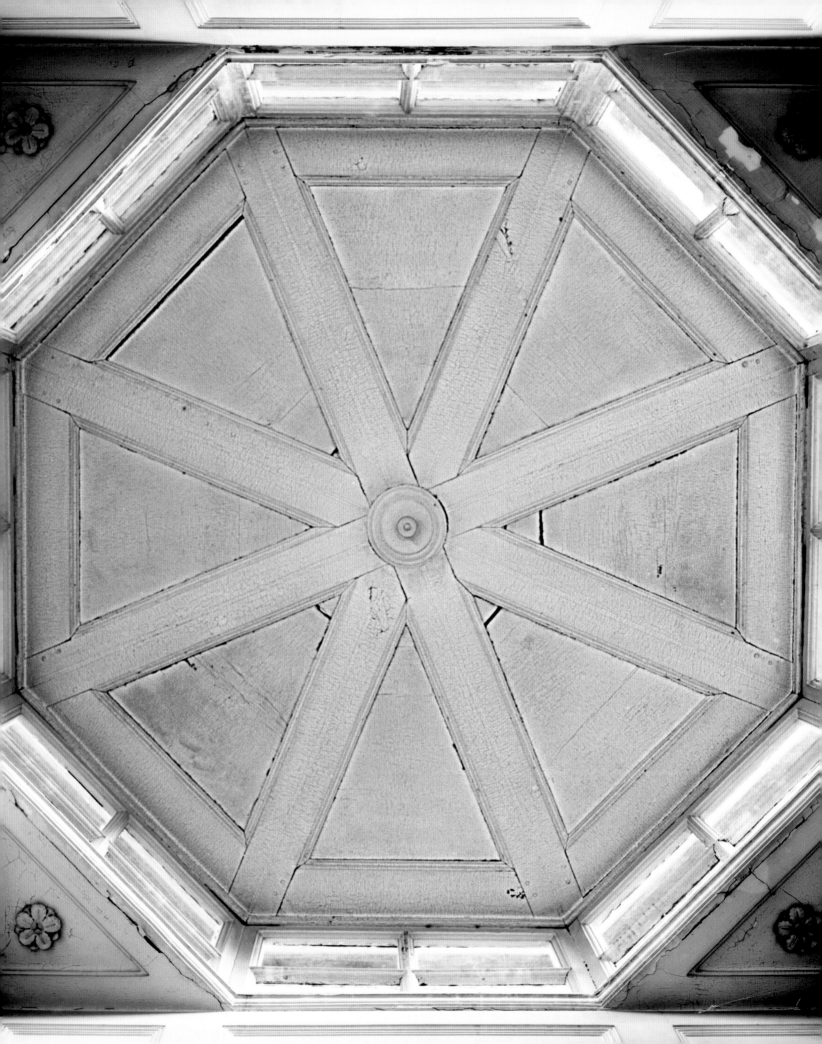

ACKNOWLEDGEMENTS

This book tells the story of our journey, the people who have helped us along the way, and the history of the house and its inhabitants, from the first Ashleys who settled there in the mid-fifteenth century right up to the present day. Justin Barton's beautiful photography has captured the magic that permeates through the building, even when things were at their lowest ebb. His images reveal the layers of history that have built up over time, the incredible craftsmanship that has been used in creating the house, and the dedication of one family to keep the place going.

There are many people I'd like to thank, without whom I could not have written this book.

My thanks go to my wife, Dinah, the love of my life, and mother of our three wonderful children, Anthony, Viva and Zara. Making this home together has been the most important decision we ever took, and I am so glad we did. I could not have done it with anyone else. You are the most precious people in the world.

Thanks to my mother for being the rock in our family. Without her perseverance, determination and foresight none of this would have been possible. She provided the foundation I needed to be able to meet this challenge head on. Thanks to my wonderful siblings Fred and Cecilia, and their respective families, for your love, support and for our incredible bond.

Thanks to Philip Rymer for his leadership and friendship, through difficult times and also through exciting ones. Thanks also to the whole estate team for enduring years of dust, debris, and noise! Thanks to Brian Stevens and Charlie Palmer-Tomkinson for their invaluable advice and support and for steering the ship through some challenging times. Thanks to Simon Elliot for all his encouragement and for always believing in me.

Thanks to Justin Barton for bringing the house alive—amazing to think it's been a decade already. Thanks to Tim Knox for his help crafting this book, for brilliantly weaving the story of my family and the house together, and for his support throughout. Thanks to Edward and Jane Hurst for guiding us every step of the way—they are an incredible double act.

Thanks to Philip Hughes and his team for overseeing the project and for introducing us to the world of building conservation. Thanks to Matthew Ellis, Sean Clarke and all the people involved from Ellis & Co., far too many to list. I promised them a book and here it is! Thanks to Nigel Cutler, Alan Riggs, Mike Burleigh, Mike Bird, John Garrick, Rick Foulkes, Malcolm Froud and the team—you all know who you are.

Thanks to Jenny Chesher and Kim Auston from Historic England for all their help and support over the years. Thanks to John Cattell and Susie Barson for the research and insights into the history of St Giles House. Thanks to Suzannah Fleming for her invaluable research of St Giles Park, and her friendship. Thanks to Adam Bates from Natural England and Chris Burnett for their help with our Parkland Plan. Thanks to Alison Verrion and Ben Eyres for looking after the landscape. Thanks to Norman Hudson from the Country Houses Foundation for his continued encouragement and support.

Thanks to Dan Annett, Historic England, *Country Life*, The Earl and Countess of Malmesbury and Viscount and Viscountess of Fitzharris for permission to use photography.

Thanks to everyone else who in some way inspired, helped, or supported us during this process.

NICK ASHLEY-COOPER
12th Earl of Shaftesbury

View looking up at the roof lantern over the main staircase of St Giles House.

page 1 Bust of the 7th Earl of Shaftesbury lying in the Stone Hall before being moved onto his plinth in the newly created entrance hall.

pages 2–3 West Pepperpot Lodge at the north entrance to St Giles Park.

pages 4–5 East elevation of pre-renovation St Giles House from the overgrown Sunk Garden.

pages 6–7 North-east view of St Giles House covered in scaffolding during renovation.

pages 8–9 A view through fields of wildflowers and the Sunk Garden to the north-east corner of St Giles House.

page 11 The family crest and motto, 'Love, Serve', is embroidered on the headboard of a four-poster bed.

page 12 A Union Jack flag, a Second World War helmet and military uniform left in the painted wardrobe in the Cecil Room.

First published in the United States of America in 2018 by Rizzoli International Publications, Inc.
300 Park Avenue South, New York, NY 10010

www.rizzoliusa.com

Copyright © 2018 by St Giles House Events

ISBN: 978-0-8478-6320-4

Library of Congress Control Number: 2018938668

For Rizzoli International Publications:
Philip Reeser, Editor
Kaija Markoe, Production Manager
Sarah Derry, Copy Editor

Designed and typeset in Sentinel by Dalrymple
Printed in China

2018 2019 2020 2021 / 10 9 8 7 6 5 4 3 2 1

IMAGE CREDITS:

All images copyright © 2018 by Justin Barton except the following:

Country Life Archive: 98 (centre), 106 (upper right)

Dan Annett: 20–21, 159, 172–73

© Historic England Archive: 18–19, 24, 28 (upper right), 40, 42, 62, 63, 74–75, 84, 85, 142, 152, 200–01, 248, 249, 250, 251

Malmesbury Archives, Hampshire Record Office: 216

Philip Hughes Associates: 43, 140–41

St Giles House Archive: 23, 26–27, 98 (top and bottom), 99, 106 (upper left), 112, 116–17, 122–23, 128–29, 142–43, 178–79, 188–89, 196, 198–99, 224, 228–29, 230, 231, 233 (top and bottom), 234, 235, 236–37

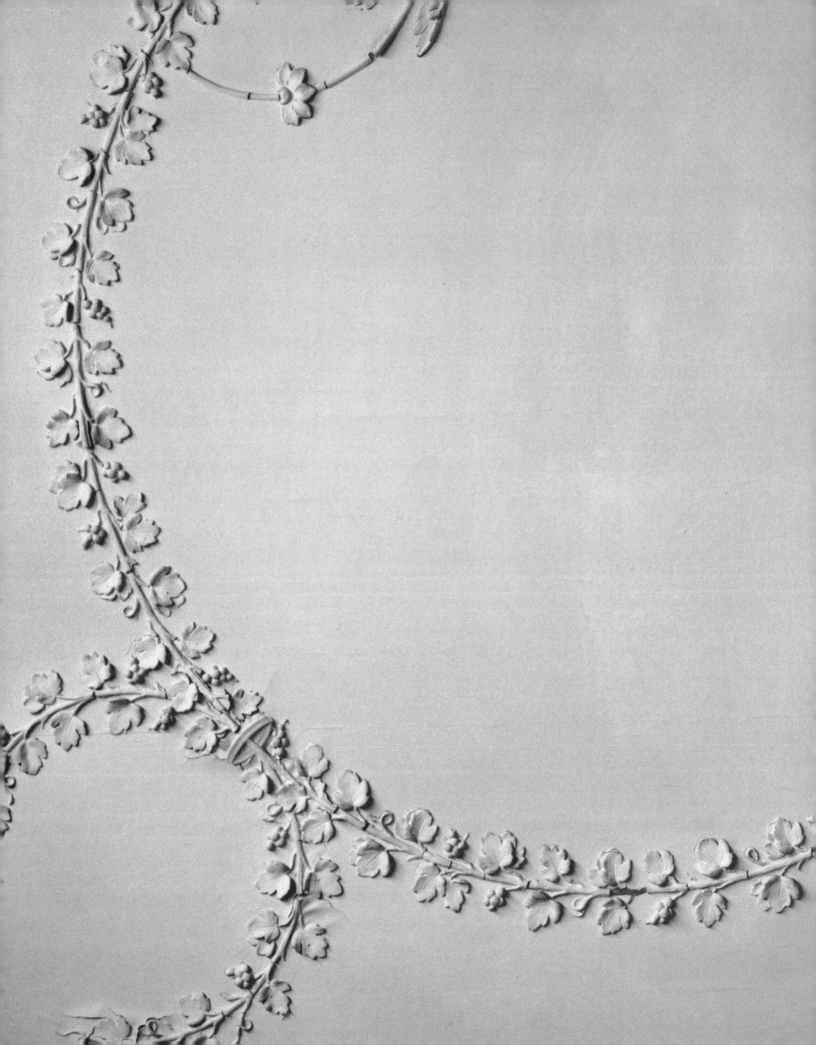